PRE-PUBLICATION REVIEWS OF LAURENCE HOULGATE'S
UNDERSTANDING DAVID HUME

"Laurence Houlgate's introduction to Hume is an admirable addition to his earlier guides to major works by Plato, Locke, Mill and Kant. The exposition is clear throughout, and readers will come away with a solid understanding of the issues Hume discusses. And because of Professor Houlgate's focus on the methods of argument and counterargument employed in the discussion of those issues, readers will also gain an appreciation for the nature of philosophical inquiry."
--J. William Forgie, Emeritus Professor of Philosophy, University of California, Santa Barbara

"With Understanding David Hume, Laurence Houlgate carefully describes and critically explains the key concepts and theories of Hume's philosophical works. He does so in a way that enables the smart student to grasp the technicalities and philosophical subtleties of Hume's reasoning. As with the previous Understanding volumes, Houlgate provides to both instructors and students an excellent resource for discussing the relevance and significance of Hume's philosophy in our time."
--Stuart Silvers, Emeritus Professor of Philosophy, Clemson University

"This book is a good introduction to Hume's philosophical method as well to his ideas concerning natural religion. Many introductory books tend to concentrate upon either methods or concepts, but not necessarily both. Recommended as a companion to Hume's Dialogues Concerning Natural Religion."
--Emily R. Gill, Caterpillar Professor of Political Science Emerita, Bradley University

"Of all Professor Houlgate's Smart Student Guides, this is my favorite. It covers interesting material in a most interesting way. Students (and other interested non-philosophers) will learn a great deal from this guide to some of Hume's most important essays."
--Merrill Ring, Emeritus Professor of Philosophy, California State University, Fullerton

Other books by Laurence Houlgate

The Smart Student's Guides to Philosophical Classics:
Understanding Plato: Socratic Dialogues and the Republic
Understanding John Locke: Second Treatise of Government
Understanding John Stuart Mill: Utilitarianism and On Liberty
Understanding Immanuel Kant: Grounding for the Metaphysics of Morals

Philosophy of the Family:
The Child and the State: A Normative Theory of Juvenile Rights
Family and State: The Philosophy of Family Law
Morals, Marriage and Parenthood: An Introduction to Family Ethics
Philosophy, Law and the Family: A New Introduction to the Philosophy of Law

UNDERSTANDING DAVID HUME

The Smart Student's Guide to *Dialogues Concerning Natural Religion*, and the essays *Of Miracles*, *Of the Immortality of the Soul*, and *Of Suicide*

With appendices containing the complete texts of the original essays

Laurence D. Houlgate

Houlgate Books
SAN LUIS OBISPO, CALIFORNIA

Copyright © 2019 by **Laurence D. Houlgate**

All rights reserved. No part of this publication may be reproduced, distributed or transmitted in any form or by any means, without prior written permission.

Houlgate Books
www.houlgatebooks.com

Book Layout © 2017 BookDesignTemplates.com
Cover by Vila Design. Viladesign.net

Understanding David Hume/ Laurence D. Houlgate. -- 1st ed.
ISBN 9781097769445

PREFACE TO THE SMART STUDENT'S GUIDE SERIES

In 1980 members of the faculty of the Philosophy Department at California Polytechnic State University were asked to create an introductory course in philosophy that would be required of every student as part of their general education. The department voted to adopt my proposal to introduce students to philosophy by having them read only the original texts of pre-20th century classics of philosophy. At least one of the texts selected for the introductory course had to be from ancient philosophy and the remainder could be from any book of philosophy published before 1900, provided that it is generally regarded as a classic and accessible to beginning students. We created two 11-week courses based on this model. One course is devoted to classic works in ethics, social and political philosophy. The other course concentrates on classic works in epistemology and metaphysics. The authors typically chosen for these courses were the usual suspects: Plato, Aristotle, Descartes, Hobbes, Locke, Rousseau, Hume, Mill, Kant, and several other of the "great" philosophers.

Our hope in adopting this approach to introducing university students to philosophy was that they would not only learn about the nature of philosophy and philosophical method, but they would leave the course having read and (hopefully) understood some of the great books in Western philosophy; a rare accomplishment in a university with an enrollment of 20,000 students, most of them specializing in science or technology.

Looking back over the past 36 years I believe we achieved the latter objective but fell short in fulfilling the former. Most students would begin a course completely ignorant of the nature of philosophy, its questions and its methods. This is quite understandable, especially in light of the fact that most students have no exposure to philosophy before enrolling in the university. And yet, although our beginning students studied, discussed and were tested on their understanding of several classic works, it occurred to me that a high proportion of them would leave our courses unable to give coherent answers to such questions as: "What is philosophy?" "What is the nature of a philosophical problem?" "What methods does the philosopher use to resolve philosophical problems?" "How does a philosophical discovery differ from a discovery in science?" If students who completed a beginning course in biology or psychology were not able to define "biology," or "psychology," remained ignorant about the unique nature of a problem in these areas of study and could not explain some of the methods used to solve these problems, then their teacher would understandably declare the course to be a failure.

I soon decided that I would use a standard to judge the success or failure of my courses similar to the standard used by my hypothetical biology or psychology colleague. I would evaluate my own classes as a success if a majority of my students showed an understanding not only of the central ideas of each philosopher discussed, but they could also explain the nature of philosophy, how philosophical questions differed from those arising in the sciences, and (especially) the unique methods used by the great philosophers to solve these problems.

Understanding David Hume is the fifth of a series of student companions to the classics of Western philosophy that attempts to achieve these modest objectives. Each book in the series organizes the central claims of each classic text with the aim of clarifying the kind of question that the philosopher is asking and the method(s) the philosopher uses in the attempt to answer that question. I make no assumptions that the kind of question asked, or the method used to answer the question will always be the same as we move from one philosopher to another. What is important is that in the attempt to clarify the questions asked by each philosopher, students will be able to identify a common thread that will allow them to say "Ah yes, this is a question that is philosophical, not scientific. It does not call for the tools or methods typically used in scientific inquiry." If questions of philosophy are not to be resolved by observational research in the field or experimentation in the laboratory, then it will be important to determine how each philosopher goes about answering the questions posed. Once again, we might be able to find a common thread that allows a student to say "There, that is how philosophers go about their work." My hope is that a critical study of the classics will show that philosophy is not after all a random enterprise in which anyone can say whatever comes into their head because they believe there is no method on which to base a rational argument.

The series title is *Smart Student's Guides to Philosophical Classics*. The series is organized into volumes distinguished by the author under consideration. The first volume presents issues and arguments in four of Plato's early ("Socratic") dialogues and in those parts of the *Republic* dealing with ethics and political philosophy. The second book is devoted to John Locke's moral and political theory in *Second Treatise of Government*. The third book is about John Stuart Mill's most famous works of philosophy: *Utilitarianism* and *On Liberty*. The fourth book is about Immanuel Kant's *Grounding for the Metaphysics of Morals*. As with previous volumes in this series, chapters in this volume (*Understanding David Hume*) will conclude with questions for thought and discussion.

Although the Smart Student's Guides can be read on their own, my hope is that they will be read as companions to the original works of the philosophers discussed therein. I certainly do not recommend the guides as a substitute for a careful reading of the classic works. Students should read the original text before looking at this or any other companion book for commentary and guidance about what the philosopher says or implies about the nature of philosophy, the important questions of philosophy and the methods of the philosopher for answering or attempting to answer these questions.

Details

Chapter sections are headed by Arabic numerals, for example: 8.1, 8.1.2, etc. Hume uses the word "Part" for "chapter." The part being discussed will be displayed in parentheses under the chapter heading, e.g. (Part III).

The page numbers following quotes cited from Hume's *Dialogues Concerning Natural Religion* refer to the R.H. Popkin edition (Hackett Publishing). This edition was selected because it is the one that is most likely to be used in contemporary English-speaking introductory philosophy courses and (most important) it is easily available at low cost. There are many other editions of Hume's book to be found in bookstores and libraries. Free downloadable copies can be found from multiple sources online (e.g., Gutenberg.org).

Quotations from Hume are indented and italicized. Names of other authors who are quoted are placed in parentheses indicating the name of the author and page number quoted, for example: (Taylor, 78). The full reference with author name, date of publication, book title, name of publisher and place of publication can be found in References, at the end of sections I, II, III and IV.

In lieu of footnotes, author comments and criticisms are placed in the body of the text, bordered by horizontal lines and printed in **boldface** font.

The original text *Of Miracles* and Hume's posthumous essays *Of Suicide* and *Of Immortality of the Soul* are reprinted in the **Appendices** section at the back of the book.

Please consult the **Glossary** for definitions of some of Hume's technical terms and other philosophical language that may not be understood by the reader.

For enthusiastic scholars, the **Bibliography** section at the back of the book contains a link to a vast trove of books and articles on the works of David Hume.

Plan of the book

The book is divided into eight sections. Section I is an introduction containing a short biography of David Hume. Section II is the student guide to *Dialogues Concerning Natural Religion*. Sections III, IV and V are guides to Hume's essays *Of Miracles*, *Of the Immortality of the Soul* and *Of Suicide*. Section VI is the author's discussion of Hume's methodology. Finally, as mentioned above, there is an appendix (Section VII) containing the original texts of the aforementioned essays, followed by Section VIII containing a glossary and a link to a bibliography of essays and books on and about Hume's work on topics related to religion.

Acknowledgements

Many thanks again to Judith Perrill Houlgate for her careful proofreading of the penultimate draft of this book. Of course, I am to blame for any typographical errors that might remain in the final draft. Thanks also to the thousands of students who attended my Philosophical Classics courses during my 51-year teaching career. Their questions and our classroom debates were of great help in the development of all of the books in this series. Finally, without the encouragement and support of my spouse, Torre Houlgate-West, it is doubtful that any of these books would have been finished.

A Modest Request

Thank you for reading *Understanding David Hume*. If you like this book, please write a short review on the book's Amazon.com detail page. For information about other books in the *Smart Student's Guides to Philosophical Classics* series, please visit my website at www.houlgatebooks.com . And feel free to comment on my occasional philosophical ramblings at: www.houlgatebooks.blogspot.com You can also write to me at my university email address: lhoulgat@calpoly.edu

For Herbert Morris

Friend and Mentor

Contents

I   INTRODUCTION 1
   1. ABOUT DAVID HUME 3
II A GUIDE TO *DIALOGUES CONCERNING NATURAL RELIGION*
.... 9
   2. ON THE EXISTENCE AND NATURE OF GOD 11
   2.1 A Challenge for Cleanthes 12
   2.2 The Design Argument 13
   2.3 Demea's Complaint 15
   2.4 A Weak Analogy 16
   2.5 Legs and Stairs 17
   2.6 Two Thought Experiments 18
   2.6.1 Abstracted Ideas of the Universe 18
   2.6.2 A First Look at the World 19
   2.6.3 Refining the Argument from Design 20
   2.7 Evaluating A Posteriori Arguments 21
   2.7.1 The Partiality Fallacy 22
   2.7.2 The Part/Whole Fallacy 23
   2.7.3 The Argument from Experience 24
   3. CLEANTHES' RESPONSE 25
   3.1 A Voice in the Clouds 25
   3.2 Books Growing on Trees 26
   4. MATERIAL AND IDEAL WORLDS 29
   5. THE EXPERIMENTAL PRINCIPLE 31
   5.1 The Finite Deity 32
   5.2 The Imperfect Deity 33
   5.3 The Deity as a Stupid Mechanic 33

5.4 A Committee of Gods 34
5.5 Procreative Gods 34
5.6 Anthropomorphic Gods 34
5.7 Summary 35
6. TOAD, TURNIP OR TOY? 37
6.1 How to Use Analogies 38
6.2 Question-begging Theories 39
7. DEMEA'S *A PRIORI* ARGUMENT 43
7.1 Necessary Existence 43
7.2 The Impossibility of Demonstrating Matters of Fact 45
7.3 Cleanthes' Rebuttal 46
8. THE PROBLEM OF EVIL 51
8.1 Examples of Evil in the World 51
8.2 The Logical Problem of Evil 52
8.3 Grasping at Straws 53
9. THE FINITELY PERFECT DEITY 55
9.1 Two Scenarios 55
9.2 There are no Unavoidable Evils 57
9.3 Demea's Angry Departure 60
10. CONFESSION AND CONFUSION 61
11. POSTSCRIPT: A HUMEAN RESPONSE TO THE
INTELLIGENT DESIGN ARGUMENT 65
Questions for thought and discussion 71
References 73
III   A GUIDE TO *OF MIRACLES* 75
12. DEFINITIONS AND STANDARDS 77
12.1 Direct Evidence 78
12.2 Hume's Definition of "Miracle" 79
12.3 Transgressions of the Law of Nature 80
12.4 Proportioning Belief to the Evidence. 80
12.5 Fallible Reasoning Concerning Matters of Fact 81

12.6 Reasoning Based on Human Testimony 82
12.7 Disputes About the Veracity of Human Testimony 83
12.8 Miracles and the Rules of Just Reasoning 84
13. THE PROBABILITY OF MIRACLES 87
13.1 Lack of Trustworthy Witnesses 87
13.2 The Misleading Role of Surprise and Wonder 88
13.3 The Contradictions of Religion 88
13.4 No Human Testimony can Prove a Miracle 90
Questions for thought and discussion 93
References 95

IV A GUIDE TO *OF THE IMMORTALITY OF THE SOUL* 97

14. IMMORTALITY: A BELIEF THAT NEVER DIES 99
14.1 What Does it Mean to Believe in Life After Death? 100
14.2 Three Arguments for Immortality 101
14.2.1 Metaphysical Arguments 102
14.2.2 Moral Arguments 105
14.2.2.1 The Injustice of Double Jeopardy 106
14.2.2.2 The Injustice of a Failure to Promulgate 107
14.2.2.3 Divine Punishment has no Purpose 108
14.2.2.4 Divine Punishment is not Proportional to the Offense ... 108
14.2.2.5 Divine Examination of Children for Possible Sins 109
14.2.2.6 Determinism and Human Responsibility 109
14.2.3 Physical arguments for Immortality 110
14.2.3.1 Proportional changes of body and mind 110
14.2.3.2 The Souls of Animals 111
14.2.3.3 The Changing Nature of the Soul 112
14.2.3.4 The Problem of Soul Disposal 112
14.3 Postscript: A Humean Response to Recent Scientific Proofs of an Afterlife 113
Questions for thought and discussion 117
References 119

V A GUIDE TO *OF SUICIDE* 121
15. IS SUICIDE IMMORAL? 123
15.1 Suicide and Duties to God 124
15.2 Suicide and Duties to Others 129
15.3 Suicide and Duties to Oneself 130
Questions for thought and discussion 133
References 135

VI PHILOSOPHICAL METHOD 137
16. HUME'S METHODOLOGY 139
16.1 The Light of Reason 139
16.2 Thought Experiments 141
16.3 Reductio ad Absurdum 141
16.4 Arguments A Priori 142
16.5 Arguments A Posteriori 144
16.6 Summary 145

VII APPENDICES 147
A. OF MIRACLES 149
B. OF THE IMMORTALITY OF THE SOUL 173
C. OF SUICIDE 181

VIII GLOSSARY AND BIBLIOGRAPHY 193

I   INTRODUCTION

DAVID HUME (1711 – 1776)

"Upon the whole, I have always considered him, both in his lifetime and since his death, as approaching as nearly to the idea of a perfectly wise and virtuous man, as perhaps the nature of human frailty will permit."

--Adam Smith

CHAPTER ONE

1. ABOUT DAVID HUME

"I have written on all sorts of subjects... yet I have no enemies; except indeed all the Whigs, all the Tories, and all the Christians."
-- David Hume

Several months before he died on August 25, 1776, David Hume penned a brief autobiography in which he revealed that he had been "struck with a disorder in my bowels, which at first gave me no alarm, but has since, as I apprehend it, become mortal and incurable" (*My Own Life*). The disorder to which he refers was probably colon cancer, but what is remarkable about Hume's final days is his positive attitude: "Notwithstanding the great decline of my person, [I] never suffered a moment's abatement of my spirits." He goes on to write that if he were to name a period of his life which he would like to repeat, "I might be tempted to point to this later period. I possess the same ardor as ever in study, and the same gaiety in company." Although he was now a man of sixty-five years, Hume explained that even if he did not have a terminal illness, he would probably have only a few more years to live anyway, battling the usual infirmities of old age.

Word had gotten out about Hume's final days and one of the many persons who came to visit was the eminent biographer James Boswell, a man who was always looking for a good story for his journals. One of Boswell's motives for visiting Hume was to try to find out whether his impending death was causing him to have a change of mind about atheism. Boswell, like his friend Dr. Johnson, was deeply religious but apparently worried that Hume might be right about death being a complete annihilation. When Boswell asked Hume whether he was afraid of this prospect, Hume responded that the thought of non-existence after death gave him "no more uneasiness" than the thought that he had not existed before death (quoting the Roman philosopher Lucretius).

Hume began his recorded existence on April 26, 1711 at Edinburgh, Scotland. His father, who passed away when David was two years old, was a descendant of a branch of the Earl of Hume's extended family. His mother was the daughter of Sir David Falconer, President of the College of Justice. But these titles did not bring great wealth to his immediate family. Moreover, proprietorship of the estate (house, grounds and a small annual income) had passed to Hume's older brother, as dictated by the ancient rules of primogeniture. David's inheritance was "very slender," amounting to £40 per year (this would be equivalent to about £8,970 or $11,946 today).

Young Hume sailed through his early education with high marks. At the age of 12 (!) he was admitted to the University of Edinburgh where he read (majored in) law and philosophy. After completing his studies while still in his teens, his mother and brother recommended the law as a perfect profession for him. He responded by telling them that the law made him "nauseous," and that he had an "unsurmountable aversion" to everything but the pursuit of philosophy and general learning.

The problem with this pursuit was that he did not have sufficient funds to be both independent and a full-time scholar. He chose dependency and spent the next several years at the family home deeply immersed in study and writing. This brought him "on the verge of a nervous breakdown" from overwork. His self-imposed therapy was to leave the family home, quit his studies and force himself to pursue a business career at Bristol, England. The change of scene appeared to work, although he greatly disliked his new life as a clerk to a sugar importer. A few months later, he made a final decision. He would devote the rest of his life to "the improvement of my life in literature," even if this decision meant that he would need "to make a very rigid frugality supply my deficiency of fortune." He found the perfect place for those who take vows of poverty: a Jesuit College in the village of La Flèche (France) where the great René Descartes had studied a century before.

It was at the college that Hume composed his first book: *A Treatise of Human Nature*. Although many modern scholars believe this to be one of the most important books in the history of philosophy, to Hume's great disappointment the book was largely ignored by the educated public, including the few eminent philosophers who were available to review it. As Hume famously said, the book "fell deadborn from the press, without reaching such distinction as even to excite a murmur among the zealots." With no career, and having depleted his funds during his three years in France, he returned once again to Scotland to live with his mother and brother and continue his studies. He was now 28 years old and still facing the same dilemma: how to support himself and also be a "man of letters."

In 1744 Hume was proposed as a candidate for the Professorship of Moral Philosophy at Edinburgh University. His application was rejected by Principal William Wishart, one of the few scholars who had read the *Treatise* but who ironically used it against Hume, maintaining that the principles therein led to "downright Atheism" (Russell). Four years later, Hume published An *Enquiry Concerning Human Understanding*. Although it was also relatively unnoticed, it "resulted in his being charged with heresy." This controversy about Hume's atheistic beliefs probably explains why he was later not selected as Chair of Logic at Glasgow University (a post that instead went to his good friend the economist Adam Smith), and why his applications were rejected for a number of other prestigious posts for which he applied (Mossner, 27).

These sad incidents and many others had a deleterious effect on Hume's ability to speak his own mind, especially in his books touching upon religious topics. Conservative clergy of the established church (Church of England) and public opinion regularly suppressed speech that threatened existing Christian dogma. It was for this reason that Hume pulled the chapter on "Miracles" from his first book, deferred publication of *Dialogues Concerning Natural Religion* until after his death and his essays "Of Suicide" and "Of the Immortality of the Soul" were withdrawn by his publisher shortly after they were printed because they had met with "violent protests...launched by leading clergymen" (Popkin, viii).

Although Hume never secured an academic position, he did manage to obtain the means to lead an independent life. He was hired as the tutor of a wealthy young nobleman ("the mad Marquess of Annandale"), a position that "came to him, as did all positions that he ever held, fortuitously" (Mossner, 26). This position was followed by: a secretaryship to a proposed military expedition in Canada; a position as aide-de-camp to a General for a secret military embassy to the Courts of Vienna and Turin; another secretaryship to the English embassy in Paris; and near the end of his life, a prestigious position as Undersecretary of State. But the post Hume most enjoyed was as Librarian at the Faculty of Advocates. Hume wrote that this post gave him "little or no emolument, but which gave me the command of a large library." He now had the time and ample resources in the library to work on his *The History of Great Britain from the Saxon Kingdoms to the Glorious Revolution*, a project he had conceived many years earlier but never had the wherewithal to complete. "This comprised a million words and took fifteen years to write, being published in six volumes between 1754 and 1762. It was well received and a commercial success" (Mossner, 28).

Hume's importance as a philosopher began to be recognized only in the final years of his life. His influence is evident in the moral philosophy and economic writings of Adam Smith. Jeremy Bentham remarked that reading Hume "caused the scales to fall" from his eyes. Charles Darwin regarded his work as a central influence on the theory of evolution. Immanuel Kant credited Hume with awakening him from his "dogmatic slumbers". But what many biographers find most extraordinary and admirable about David Hume was his stubborn refusal to give up on his boyhood dream to lead a life of research and writing, despite the constant need early on to provide for the bare necessities of food and shelter. Although he excelled in all of his nonacademic pursuits, he once wrote that "Had I been born to a small estate in Scotland of a hundred a year, I should have remained at home all my life, planted and improved my fields, read my book, and wrote philosophy..." (Greig, 188).

References

Greig, J.Y.T. 2011. The Letters of David Hume, volume 2. Oxford: Oxford University Press.

Hume, David. 1776. "My Own Life", in Norton, D.F. (ed.) The Cambridge Companion to Hume. 1993. Cambridge: Cambridge University Press.

Jessop, T.E. 1966. A Bibliography of David Hume and of Scottish Philosophy. New York: Russell and Russell.

Lucretius, ca 50 BCE. De Rerum Natura.
http://www2.gsu.edu/~phltso/deathfrags.html

Morris, William Edward and Brown, Charlotte R., 2017. "David Hume", The Stanford Encyclopedia of Philosophy (Spring 2017 Edition), Edward N. Zalta(ed.),
https://plato.stanford.edu/archives/spr2017/entries/hume/.

Mossner, E.C. 1968, "Philosophy and Biography: The Case of David Hume", Chappell, V.C. (ed.) Hume. Notre Dame and London: University of Notre Dame Press.

Hampshire, S.N. 1963. "Hume's Place in Philosophy" in Pears, D.F. (ed.) David Hume: A Symposium. London: Macmillan.

Popkin, Richard H. 1998. "Introduction", Dialogues Concerning Natural Religion, Second Edition. Indianapolis: Hackett.

Russell, Paul. 1997. "Wishart, Baxter and Hume's Letter from a Gentleman" Hume Studies. Volume XXIII, Number 2: 245-276. http://www.humesociety.org/hs/issues/v23n2/russell/russell-v23n2.pdf

Schwartz, Richard B. 1991. Boswell and Hume: the deathbed interview. Cambridge University Press. https://www.cambridge.org/core/books/new-light-on-boswell/boswell-and-hume-the-deathbed-interview/0D8E152BD8E6B10EB738C899E07D5238

Williams, B.A.O. 1963. "Hume on Religion" in Pears, D.F. (ed.) David Hume: A Symposium. London: Macmillan.

II A GUIDE TO *DIALOGUES CONCERNING NATURAL RELIGION*

CHAPTER TWO

2. ON THE EXISTENCE AND NATURE OF GOD

(*Dialogues*, Part II)

The opening scene is the library in the home of Demea, one of three main characters in the dialogue. The other participants are Cleanthes and Philo. The entire dialogue is reported to us by a fourth character, Pamphilus, a young student of Cleanthes, who was urged by his friends to put down in writing what was said on that imaginary but auspicious day.

The dialogue form used by Hume is not unusual. It was certainly the favorite vehicle for Plato and for several Greek and Roman authors. It is believed that Hume was inspired to use this form by Cicero's dialogue The Nature of the Gods.

Readers will probably be pleased to know that the commentary that follows is not in dialogue form. Instead, what each character says will be reported and commented on in each chapter, but only when this is relevant to the progress of an argument or counterargument. This will hopefully be accomplished in language that is more understandable for beginning students than the frequent lengthy speeches and (sometimes) elaborate literary words and phrases that Hume wrote for his characters. Each chapter is divided into discrete parts that are labeled in such a way that the reader can easily locate arguments and topics that they would like to target for re-examination.

As the title indicates, *Dialogues Concerning Natural Religion* (hereafter referred to as *Dialogues*) is about natural as opposed to revealed religion. Revealed religion is a set of beliefs about the existence and commands of a god that have been revealed by the god to human beings. Natural religion, by contrast, means religious beliefs that are supported by scientific evidence and rational reasoning.

Readers will notice that this chapter begins with Parts II and III of *Dialogues*. Part I is omitted because the polite discussion taking place therein is about the "unexciting question of whether students should be taught the principles of religion at the beginning or end of their formal education" (Popkin, x). This is clearly not the question that attracts most readers to Hume's *Dialogues*. The questions that draw attention and dominate the discussion between the three friendly combatants are: "What is the nature of God?" and "Can experience and observation be of any help in discovering God's essential attributes?"

2.1 A Challenge for Cleanthes

Demea begins the dialogue with the remark that no one "of common sense" has ever entertained a serious doubt about the existence of God. Philo agrees and backs up his concurrence with this brief argument: "Nothing exists without a cause; and the original cause of this universe (whatever it is) we call God, and piously ascribe to him every species of perfection" (14).

In the philosophy of religion, this argument is a short version of what is now called the Cosmological Argument for the existence of God. It is one of two types of argument discussed in the dialogue, the other being the Design Argument. The distinction that Hume makes between these arguments is explained in the next section (2.2).

Although Philo thinks that this argument is "unquestionable and self-evident," he quickly adds that there is no basis or reason for thinking that the perfections of God have any resemblance to such human qualities as wisdom, thought, strength, or benevolence. Our human ideas do not correspond to God's perfections, nor do his attributes "have any resemblance to these qualities among men. He is infinitely superior to our limited view and comprehension" (14). We can imagine a human being to be very wise and very strong, but we cannot even begin to imagine what it would be like to be infinitely wise and infinitely strong. And so it is with all of the perfections which are commonly attributed to God.

In his reply to Philo's grand pronouncements, Cleanthes rises to the challenge. He says that he can "prove at once the existence of the deity and his similarity to human mind and intelligence" (Part III, 15). This sudden diversion from the Cosmological argument will continue for the next five chapters. We will return to a critical discussion of it and related arguments for God's existence in Chapter 7.

2.2 The Design Argument

Cleanthes begins by asking Philo and Demea to "look round the world." He proclaims that when we do so, it should be obvious that there is a remarkable resemblance between natural objects (animals, minerals, vegetables) and objects designed and produced by human beings (houses, carriages, watches). The resemblance is to be found in "the curious adapting of means to ends." Cleanthes thinks it obvious that the natural world is "nothing but one great machine subdivided into an infinite number of lesser machines, which again admit of subdivisions to a degree beyond what human senses and faculties can trace and explain." (15) These natural machines resemble exactly, though [they] much exceed, the productions of human contrivance:

> *Since, therefore, the effects resemble each other, we are led to infer by all the rules of analogy, that the causes also resemble, and that the Author of Nature is somewhat similar to that of the mind of man, though possessed of much larger faculties, proportioned the grandeur of the work which he has executed (14).*

This is Cleanthes' first statement of the Design Argument for the existence and nature of the Deity. Cleanthes refers to it as an a posteriori argument and says that it proves "at once the existence of the Deity and his similarity to human mind and intelligence."

A posteriori arguments are founded on experience and attempt to prove the *probability* of the conclusion (this type of argument is also referred to as "inductive"). In this respect the Design Argument differs from Philo's previous a priori argument (2.1) which attempted to prove the *certainty* of the conclusion (this type of argument is also referred to as "deductive"). And yet, both arguments begin with a factual claim. Philo begins with the premise "Nothing exists without a cause." Cleanthes begins with the premise "Things in the natural world and the productions of human contrivance both display a curious adapting of means to ends."

One type of a posteriori argument is analogical. It has the following form:

1. A, B, C and D have properties or attributes p, q and r in common.
2. A, B and C also have property or attribute s.
3. Therefore, D probably has property or attribute s.

The conclusion (3) is inferred from premises (1) and (2) with probability, not certainty. It is logically possible that D might have the same attributes (p, q, r) as A, B and C but D does not have the attribute s. (For example, if Jones and Smith both have the same symptoms, it is possible that they do not have the same disease).

Cleanthes argument (quoted above) is clearly analogical. It states in the first premise (below) that there is a similarity between things in the natural world (animals, vegetables, minerals) and artifacts (houses, bicycles, computers).

1. Things in the natural world and the productions of human contrivance have in common "the curious adapting of means to ends."
2. The productions of human contrivance have the further attribute of being designed and manufactured by beings who have the attributes of thought, wisdom and intelligence.
3. Therefore, things in the natural world are (probably) designed and created by a being who has thought, wisdom and intelligence, that is, God, Deity, or Author of Nature.

In premise (1), Cleanthes uses the words "curious adapting of means to ends" to show that things in the natural world, like artifacts ("machines") have parts that are so arranged that under proper conditions, they work together to serve a certain end or purpose (Rowe, 57). For example, the human eye, like a watch or a bicycle, has parts ("means") that are so arranged that they work together for a certain purpose ("end"). The parts of a watch enable a person to tell the time of day. The parts of the eye enable a person to see. If we accept this analogy, then it is a short step to the conclusion (3) that the probable cause of the things we see in the natural world is an intelligent being (God).

2.3 Demea's Complaint

Demea immediately expresses outrage not only by a conclusion that endorses "the similarity of the Deity to men," but also the "medium" by which the conclusion is established. The medium to which he refers is an argument a posteriori that establishes only probability to the conclusion. Demea believes that proofs a priori provide a much stronger basis for belief in a deity because such proofs promise certainty. He demands that future arguments for the existence and nature of the deity should concentrate entirely on a priori arguments (see Chapter 7, below).

2.4 A Weak Analogy

Philo ignores the plea of Demea to discuss only a priori arguments. Instead of dismissing the a posteriori analogical approach of Cleanthes, as requested by Demea, Philo continues to focus on the Design Argument. He argues that Cleanthes' presentation of the argument gives only "a very weak analogy" because the similarity of the natural world to the artificial is "much less than exact" (16).

Philo shows the weakness of the analogy with a counter-argument that leads to the conclusion that the universe must have had a designer because of the absurd comparison of the universe to a house. We know that the houses we observe had an architect or builder "because this is precisely that species of effect which we have experienced to proceed from that species of cause." In other words, experience teaches us that houses are the product of human design and production because all the houses we have ever seen have this kind of cause. We have no experience of houses growing on trees or of animals giving birth to houses. But when we gaze at night at the nearest galaxy, few would say "The universe looks exactly like a house. It must have been designed and built by an intelligent being."

> *"The dissimilitude is so striking that the utmost you can here pretend to is a guess, a conjecture, a presumption concerning a similar cause." (16)*

Unlike the multiple experiences we have had of houses, and of their designers and builders, we have no experiences at all of universes, no "species of effect" which is known from past experience to have proceeded from an intelligent designer.

It is one thing to believe that the universe contains many parts, each of which represents a "curious adapting of means to ends." But it is quite another thing to believe that the universe itself has a purpose or end in which suns and planets are the means to achieving this mysterious purpose. Do planets constitute a "part" of the universe? What is the purpose of the universe? How do the parts serve this purpose?

2.5 Legs and Stairs

Cleanthes denies that the dissimilarity is that extreme. He argues that the "whole adjustment of means to ends in a house and in the universe" should not be dismissed as a "slight resemblance." In both the house and the universe we find "order, proportion and arrangement of every part." He turns to another analogy to prove this point:

> *Steps of a stair are plainly contrived that human legs may use them in mounting; and this inference is certain and infallible. Human legs are also contrived for walking and mounting; and this inference, I allow is not altogether so certain because of the dissimilarity which you remark; but does it, therefore, deserve the name only of presumption or conjecture? (16)*

–

Cleanthes is here attempting to turn the tables on Philo by presenting an argument that he hopes is more persuasive. Instead of using an analogy between the universe and a house, his analogy is between human legs and steps of a stair. If steps of a stair are contrived for mounting, then the similarity of human legs to steps

of a chair makes it likely that human legs are also contrived for mounting.

2.6 Two Thought Experiments

Shortly after this remark there is another interruption by Demea. He accuses Philo of assenting to "these extravagant opinions of Cleanthes." Philo responds that Demea "does not seem to apprehend" that he is arguing with Cleanthes "in his own way, by showing him the dangerous consequences of his tenets." Demea responds that Philo and Cleanthes run the risk of coming to the unacceptable conclusion that there is no viable argument for the existence and nature of God. Philo tries to calm Demea by restating the a posteriori argument of Cleanthes. He offers two thought experiments.

A thought experiment is an experiment of the mind or imagination. It is usually employed in philosophy to disprove a theory or principle by showing that it leads to an unacceptable or contradictory conclusion.

2.6.1 Abstracted Ideas of the Universe

Suppose you are asked to contemplate your ideas (concepts), abstracted from everything you know or have ever seen. Cleanthes asserts that this contemplation would tell you nothing about "what kind of scene the universe must be" nor would it give you any basis for saying that any particular scene is to be preferred to any other. It is not logically impossible or a contradiction to say that the universe is made up of only one galaxy and one planet inhabited by humans, trolls, gnomes and dwarves, and there is no necessity in conceiving of the universe as we now find it, that is, a universe made up of billions of galaxies, including the galaxy containing our planet earth. Philo tells Demea that

> ...*every chimera of [your] fancy would be upon an equal footing; nor could [you] assign any just reason why [you] adhere to one idea or system, and reject the others which are equally possible.*

These remarks have implications for a later discussion of religious systems. If we can clearly conceive of a monotheistic system in which the world is created and governed by one god, then we can also conceive of a polytheistic system in which the world is governed by many gods. Both conceptions are on an "equal footing" with each other. Perhaps of more importance, it might also be claimed that there is no logical impossibility in the idea of a system in which the universe has not been created and designed by an intelligent being.

2.6.2 A First Look at the World

Philo introduces another thought experiment. Suppose you open your eyes for the first time and look at the world as it really is. The first thing you see is a volcano spewing rocks and ash into the air. If asked, you would not be able to "assign a cause" to this event because "experience alone can point out the true cause..." (17). If you have had no previous experience of volcanic eruptions, then any cause of it that you suggest would be an arbitrary guess.

Moreover, the fact that we see "order, arrangement, or the adjustment of final causes, is not itself any proof of design, but only so far as it has been experienced to proceed from that principle" (17). We have no more difficulty in conceiving a priori that the "exquisite arrangement" we see in the elements of matter (for example, in a crystal) has "the source or spring of order originally within itself," than conceiving that the ideas of matter in "a great universal mind" spring from some unknown source of order within it.

2.6.3 Refining the Argument from Design

Continuing with this line of argument, Philo says that Cleanthes may be on to something. Experience teaches us that there is a difference between the *parts of an artifact* and *the idea of an artifact* in a human mind. Compare a watch or a house with the plan of a watch or a house:

> *Throw several pieces of steel together, without shape or form; they will never arrange themselves so as to compose a watch. Stone and mortar and wood, without an architect, never erect a house. But the ideas in the human mind, we see, by an inexplicable economy, arrange themselves so as to form the plan of a watch or a house (18).*

It is the plan of a house that causes the existence of the house. "From similar effects we infer similar causes" (17). The similar effects are the house and the universe. Hence, it is highly probable that the causes of both are similar. It is in the plan (idea) of the universe in the mind of an intelligent being that we are to find the cause of the universe.

We know by experience two things. First, we know that the pieces of watch do not arrange themselves into a watch. Second, ideas in the human mind can and do arrange themselves into a plan of a watch.

From these two kinds of experience we can draw the conclusion that "there is an original principle of order in the mind, not in matter."

If we accept the principle that "from similar effects we infer similar causes," and we also accept that the adjustment of means to ends is to be found in both natural objects and artifacts, we can plausibly conclude that the causes of each are similar. The dog, the tree, the crystal and indeed, the universe itself are ultimately the product of intelligent design. In the same way that the plan of an intelligent being is the cause of a house or a watch, so the plan of an intelligent being is the cause of the universe.

2.7 Evaluating A Posteriori Arguments

Philo summarizes the preceding argument (2.5.3) by pointing out that there is no dispute about the following principles of reasoning: (a) All inferences concerning fact are founded on experience; and (b) all experimental reasonings are founded on the supposition that similar causes prove similar effects. Philo had earlier said that if we infer that "a stone will fall, that fire will burn, that the earth has solidity," it is because "we have observed [these phenomena] a thousand and a thousand times" (16). If we set up an experiment to prove that a lit cigarette will probably cause a fire if dropped in dry brush, "the exact similarity" of this case to previous cases in which fires have been the result of incendiary devices provides us with strong evidence for our hypothesis.

Philo warns that "all just reasoners" must proceed with caution "in the transferring of experiments to similar cases":

> *Unless the cases be exactly similar, they repose no perfect confidence in applying their past observation to any particular phenomenon. Every alteration of circumstances occasions a doubt concerning the event; and it requires new experiments to prove certainly that the new circumstances are of no moment or importance. A change in bulk, situation, arrangement, age,*

> *disposition of the air, or surrounding bodies; any of these particulars may be attended with the most unexpected consequences (18).*

In the dropped cigarette example mentioned above, the inference that the brush will catch fire will be challenged if the brush is wet or if the cigarette is dropped on a windless day. New experiments must be conducted using dry brush and wind.

This cautionary remark prompts Philo to ask Cleanthes whether he had taken too wide a step "when you compared to the universe houses, ships, furniture, machines; and, from their similarity in some circumstances, inferred a similarity in their causes?" (19). Philo suggests that there are two fallacies of reasoning that Cleanthes has made in offering his analogy: (a) being partial for intelligence as the cause of the universe, and (b) making the assumption that the type of cause found in one part of the universe will also be the type of cause of the entire universe.

2.7.1 The Partiality Fallacy

Philo points out that there are many more "springs and principles of the universe" than thought, design and intelligence (19). Known active causes at work in nature are "heat and cold, attraction or repulsion and a hundred others which fall under daily observation". It is true that intelligence is "an active cause by which some particular parts of nature, we find, produce alterations on other parts." But it is only one active cause among many others!

> *What peculiar privilege has this little agitation of the brain which we call "thought", that we must thus make it the model of the whole universe? Our partiality in our own favor does indeed present it on all occasions, but sound philosophy ought carefully to guard against so natural an illusion (19).*

We choose thought and design as the cause of the universe because we have observed that this is how humans create objects or make changes to objects. But we have also observed many other sources of creation and change, for example, freezing can cause unprotected water pipes to expand and break. "When water freezes, its molecules crystalize into an open hexagonal form, which takes up more space than when the molecules are in their liquid form — that is, the water molecules expand as they freeze." Shall we conclude from this phenomenon that the universe was created by the natural force of freezing? Of course not, but in lieu of scientific investigation, this conclusion is no less credible than the conclusion that the universe was created by an intelligent designer.

And if it is argued that a hexagonal shape could only have been created by an intelligent designer, this begs the question: "How do you know this?" The answer could not be: "By observation of the formation of crystals" because experience teaches us that the "natural force of freezing" is one cause among many possible causes of the hexagonal shape.

2.7.2 The Part/Whole Fallacy

Philo has a second point to make about the way in which bias for human causation can lead us to make unsupported conclusions about the cause of the universe. Although we know by observation that humans "possess thought, intelligence, reason, or anything similar to these faculties…," we have no ground for thinking that the inhabitants on other planets possess similar faculties (19).

> *And if thought, as we may well suppose, be confined merely to this narrow corner, and has even there so limited a sphere of action, with what propriety can we assign it for the original*

> *cause of all things? ...A very small part of this great system, during a very short time, is very imperfectly discovered to us; and do we thence pronounce decisively the origin of the whole? (19-20)*

2.7.3 The Argument from Experience

Philo concludes his lengthy discourse with a reminder about the "argument from experience":

> *When two species of objects have always been observed to be conjoined together, I can infer, by custom, the existence of one wherever I see the existence of the other. (20)*

Ships and cities are conjoined to human contrivance. This we know from experience. If we come upon a ship that we have never seen before, we can plausibly conclude that it has been designed and constructed by human beings. But we have no experience of the origin of worlds or universes. We certainly have not seen any worlds being created by intelligent designers, "and it is not sufficient surely, that we have seen ships and cities arise from human art and contrivance." (21) Philo challenges Cleanthes to show a plausible similarity between the fabrication of a house and the generation of a universe:

> *Have worlds ever been formed under your eye, and have you had leisure to observe the whole progress of the phenomenon, from the first appearance of order to its final consummation? If you have, then cite your experience, and deliver your theory. (22)*

CHAPTER THREE

3. CLEANTHES' RESPONSE

(*Dialogues*, Part III)

Cleanthes arises to the challenge by presenting Philo and Demea with a counter argument based on two of his own thought experiments

3.1 A Voice in the Clouds

Cleanthes asks us to imagine hearing a loud, melodious, articulate voice that seems to come from the clouds. It is unlike any voice that we have ever heard:

> *Suppose that this voice [was] extended in the same instant over all nations and spoke to each nation in its own language and dialect; suppose that the words delivered not only contain a just sense and meaning but convey some instruction altogether worthy of a benevolent Being superior to mankind. (23)*

Cleanthes argues that we would not hesitate to ascribe the cause of this voice to "some design or purpose" any more than we would not hesitate to infer the cause of an articulate voice that we hear in a dark room to be that of a human being. In making this ascription, we would reject any complaint that there is "little analogy" between this extraordinary voice and a human voice because the former voice is loud, heard by everyone on earth, and heard in all languages. It would be absurd to conjecture that this voice was "some accidental whistling of the winds, not from any divine reason or intelligence." (24)

3.2 Books Growing on Trees

In a second thought experiment Cleanthes asks us to imagine two things: (1) There is a natural, universal, invariable language, common to every individual of the human race, and (2) books are natural productions which perpetuate themselves in the same manner with animals and vegetables, by descent and propagation. There are animals that give birth to books, and there are trees that grow books.

Cleanthes argues that if we entered our library "thus peopled by natural volumes containing the most refined reason and most exquisite beauty," we would not doubt that the "original cause" of these books is mind and intelligence. We would ignore the fact that the books are propagated by animals or grow like fruit on trees.

> *Could you persist, in asserting that all this, at the bottom, had really no meaning, and that the first formation of this volume in the loins of its original parent proceed not from thought and design? (24)*

Cleanthes gives Philo a choice: either a rational volume is no proof of an intelligent cause or all the works of nature have a similar cause. If the former, then we would have to embrace the absurdity that some books might have grown on trees, without any help from an intelligent designer. Hence, we must choose the latter option: all the works of nature have a cause similar to the cause of a book: intelligent design. Consider, for example, the human eye. If we "anatomize" and "survey its structure and contrivance," we cannot help but conclude that the eye is ultimately the product of a contriver. In fact, the anatomy of an animal "affords many stronger instances of design" than the perusal of a book.

Demea interrupts at this point, not to object to Cleanthes' conclusion about the existence of a Deity, but to point out that his argument wrongly suggests that "we comprehend the Deity and have some adequate idea of his nature and attributes" (26). Cleanthes has not given us any reason for concluding that the Deity has a mind similar to that of human beings. Demea concludes with this remark:

> *By representing the Deity as so intelligible and comprehensible, and so similar to a human mind, we are guilty of the grossest and most narrow partiality, and make ourselves the model of the whole universe* (27).

CHAPTER FOUR

4. MATERIAL AND IDEAL WORLDS

(*Dialogues,* Part IV)

Philo gives some support to Demea's objection when he offers a proof that "there is no ground to suppose a plan of the world to be formed in the Divine Mind, consisting of distinct ideas, differently arranged, in the same manner as an architect forms in his head the plan of a house which he intends to execute" (30). If there is such a plan, then "we are still obliged to mount higher in order to find the cause of this cause (the plan of an Ideal World found in the Divine Mind)" which Cleanthes "had assigned as satisfactory and conclusive" (30).

Philo continues this line of reasoning when he asks why those who believe in an Author of Nature should be satisfied by stopping at an Ideal World into which they trace the material. "If the material world rests upon a similar ideal world, this ideal world must rest upon some other, and so on without end" (31). Why not stop at the material world? There is no contradiction in asserting that the material world contains "the principle of order" within itself. And to say that the order of causes and effects has no beginning and no ending should give no more satisfaction than simply asserting that this order stops at the material world.

The preceding argument has the following structure. Let us assume that the material world is the known universe. Either (1) the parts of the material world fall into order of themselves and by their own nature, or (2) the parts of the material world are ordered by an Author of the material world. The fallacy is to declare that (1) is false, thereby affirming (2). But there is nothing to support the claim that (1) is false.

> *We have, indeed, experience of ideas which fall into order of themselves and without any known cause. But... we have a much larger experience of matter which does the same, as in all instances of generation and vegetation ... (31).*

For example, there are many instances in which an inventor is asked "How did you come up with that idea?" and the inventor answers: "I don't know. It just came to me." Matter in the form of animals and vegetables presents the same puzzle. The cat gives birth to kittens and the tree sheds seeds that develop into mighty oaks. The eighteenth-century scientist is at a loss to explain how matter "falls into order" of itself to do these acts of reproduction "without any known cause."

CHAPTER FIVE

5. THE EXPERIMENTAL PRINCIPLE

(*Dialogues*, Part V)

Philo begins this part of the dialogue by reminding Cleanthes of the experimental principle: "Like effects prove like causes." It is important that Cleanthes understands that the principle is an *argument* which is made stronger by the number of like effects and is weakened when the effects are few and/or are not alike. When a physician diagnoses lung cancer as the cause of her patient's symptoms, she wants to see as many relevant like effects as possible to support her conclusion. Although the physician knows that her patient will be distressed by the bad news, it is the experimental principle/argument that ultimately guides the diagnosis.

Philo is not objecting to the use of analogies. Instead, he wants to emphasize the difference between strong and weak analogies. In the following quote, Hume applies this caution to a second version of the principle: "Like causes proves like effects":

> *Where the causes are entirely similar, the analogy is perfect, and the inference, drawn from it, is regarded as certain and conclusive* [that is, highly probable] ...*But where the objects have not so exact a similarity, the analogy is less perfect, and the inference is less conclusive; though still it has some force, in proportion to the degree of similarity and resemblance* (Hume, *Enquiry*, 104)

Philo uses the first version of the experimental principle to show Cleanthes that despite what he wants to believe about the Deity, analogies between the world and human contrivances lead to conclusions about the nature of the Deity that are absurd or otherwise unacceptable to any committed theist.

Philo is here employing the time-honored tactic called reductio ad absurdum in which an argument is disproven by following its implications logically to an unacceptable conclusion. The fallacy is in the Design Argument itself in which it is claimed that the world as we know it offers sufficient proof of an infinite, perfect Deity. Philo proves that on the contrary, the world as we know it would offer the opposite result: a finite, imperfect god or a committee of gods who have delivered a botched design and in which it is not even known whether this god (gods) created the world they presumably designed. Indeed, Philo emphasizes, we cannot even know from the Design Argument whether God is dead or alive.

5.1 The Finite Deity

When it is said that God is infinite the theist means that God has no finite limits in time, space, power, goodness, and intelligence. God has no temporal beginning or ending, no boundaries, and is omnipotent, omniscient and all-good.

Philo's first reductio is about the alleged "infinity" of the Deity. The question is whether there is anything about the world that humans inhabit that would prove that it is the creation of an infinite God. If we apply the experimental principle to this question, then we must begin with the proposition that like effects prove like causes. Assume that the effects are those that we observe around us as we contemplate human beings, objects and events in the world. These effects are decidedly not perfect. We see many finitely intelligent, good, powerful people residing in finite space and time. If "the cause ought only to be proportioned to the effect, and the effect, so far as it falls under our cognizance, is not infinite," then there is no basis for ascribing infinite attributes to the Divine Being. He or she has the same finite attributes possessed by most human beings.

5.2 The Imperfect Deity

Philo uses a nearly identical argument to prove that contrary to Cleanthes' claims about the attributes of the Deity, the experimental argument does not prove that the Deity is perfect in any of the ways usually claimed, whether or not we assume that the Deity is infinite. Again, the relevant effect of the Divine Author is the world that we see around us. We have no standard for saying that what we see is perfect or imperfect.

> *"It is impossible for us to tell, from our limited views, whether this system contains any great faults or deserves any considerable praise if compared to other possible and even real systems"* (36).

If the comparison shows that there are great faults in our world, then the blame should be placed on the alleged creator of that world, exactly as we would do when we find out that the new car we just bought is a "lemon," frequently in the repair shop after each breakdown.

5.3 The Deity as a Stupid Mechanic

The experimental argument also proves that a perfect world does not imply a perfect craftsman. The "complicated, useful and beautiful" ship we see in the harbor could have been built by a "stupid mechanic" who was following the design of many others who had learned their craft over centuries of ship building. By analogy, the universe may have been created by a "stupid Deity" who built the world from a plan slowly improved upon and passed down to him through several generations. Philo's point is that it is more likely that the Deity who made the universe was a mere mechanic imitating the work of architects who had died long ago than that the universe was produced by a Deity from his/her unique design.

> *In such subjects ["world-making"] who can determine where the truth, nay, who can conjecture where the probability lies, amidst a great number of hypotheses which may be proposed, and a still greater which may be imagined?* (36)

5.4 A Committee of Gods

Philo reminds Cleanthes that if he takes the experimental principle seriously, then experience teaches us that the artifacts produced here on earth are more likely to be designed and created by many persons, not one. Hence, a fourth result of the experimental argument is the implication that many deities, not one, worked together to create the universe. This polytheistic result is a direct contradiction of monotheism, which preaches that there is only one God.

5.5 Procreative Gods

Human beings are created through the process of procreation, "and this is common to all living creatures." Why, then would we refuse to admit that the "numerous and limited deities" might also renew their species by generation?

5.6 Anthropomorphic Gods

Whether there is one god or many, we must admit the high probability that they have a human shape, with "eyes, a nose, mouth, ears, etc." (37). The relevant experimental argument leading to this conclusion is obvious. Quoting Epicurus, Philo says since "no one has ever seen reason but in a human figure; therefore, the gods must have a human figure." (37)

5.7 Summary

The question is "What is the nature of the deity? What attributes does God possess?" If we assume that this question can only be answered by (what Philo calls) the experimental argument, then we must apply the principle "Like effects prove like causes." The effects mentioned by Cleanthes are natural things (plants and animals) and artifacts (machines). If these effects resemble each other (if they are alike), then it is inferred that their causes also resemble each other. Thus, if the human brain resembles a computer, and we know that computers are designed and produced by intelligent beings, then we can infer that the human brain is probably also designed and produced by an intelligent being or intelligent beings. Let us recall that the question is about the *nature* of this intelligent being, not about his or her existence. It is to this question that Philo replies that the experimental argument proves that it is more likely that it is not one but several intelligent beings who created the universe itself and the natural objects in the universe. Each of these designers and creators have attributes (strength, intelligence) that are finite. Some of these gods are imperfect designers and builders, born from and eventually pro-creators of other beings of their species who would probably look remarkably like human beings. In sum, the experimental argument for the nature of god or gods gives more support to the polytheistic religions of the ancient Greeks with their finite and imperfect gods than it does to the theistic religions of Muslims, Christians and Jews who herald the existence of one God of infinite perfection.

CHAPTER SIX

6. TOAD, TURNIP OR TOY?

(*Dialogues*, Parts VI & VII)

Philo introduces a new idea which he says will "subvert" all of Cleanthes' reasoning, and destroy even the first inferences on which he "reposes such confidence." (44) The new idea is that "the universe bears a greater likeness to animal bodies and to vegetables than to the works of human art." In fact, Philo continues,

> ...*it is more probable that its cause resembles the cause of the former than that of the latter, and its origin ought rather to be ascribed to generation or vegetation than to reason or design.* (44).

Demea is the first to respond to this proposal. He asks how the world can come to exist "from anything similar to vegetation or generation." (45) Philo responds:

> *In like manner as a tree sheds its seed into the neighboring fields and produces other trees, so the great vegetable, the world, or this planetary system produces within itself certain seeds which, being scattered into the surrounding chaos, vegetate into new worlds... Or if...we should suppose this world to be an animal; a comet is the egg of this animal; and in like manner as an ostrich lays its egg in the sand, which without any care, hatches the egg and produces a new animal...* (45)

Does the universe resemble a toad or a turnip more than it resembles a man-made toy? Demea strongly objects to an affirmative answer to this question as "wild, arbitrary suppositions." He complains that animals and vegetables are "so widely different" from the world, having such a "slight, imaginary resemblance" to it, that they cannot "establish the same inference with regard to both." (45)

"Right," cries Philo:

> *This is the topic on which I have all along insisted. I have still asserted that we have no data to establish any system of cosmogony. Our experience, so imperfect in itself and so limited both in extent and duration, can afford us no provable conjecture concerning the whole of things.* (45)

When asked "What is the cause of the universe?" we have no more rational basis for answering "The Great Designer," than we have for saying "The Great Animal" or "The Great Vegetable." The best answer is "I don't know."

6.1 How to Use Analogies

If we are going to use an analogy to support a hypothesis about the origin of the world, then there is no other standard "than the great similarity of the objects compared."

> *And does not a plant or animal, which springs from vegetation or generation, bear a stronger resemblance to the world than does any artificial machine which arises from reason and design?* (45)

Demea does not answer this question. Instead, he asks Philo to explain "the operations" of vegetation and generation. Philo sidesteps this question and insists that the only thing important at this point of the discussion is that "when I see an animal, I infer that it sprang from generation; and that with as great a certainty as you conclude a house to have been reared by design." (46) We may be mystified by the process, that is, we may not understand how generation produces animals, but neither do we understand how reason (design) produces houses. The effects (animals and houses) are known, and one of these principles (generation, reason), more than the other "has no privilege for being a standard to the whole of nature." (46). There is nothing in our experience of seeing animals grow and houses being built that allows us to prefer reason instead of generation (or vice versa) as an explanation of the origin of the world.

Philo claims that there are four principles which are the known causes of similar effects "in this little corner of the world alone." These principles (causes) are reason, instinct, generation, and vegetation (46). Philo makes three observations about them. First, there may be thousands of other types of principles to be found in the "immense extent and variety of the universe." Second, any one of these principles "may afford us a theory by which to judge of the origin of the world." Third, "it is a palpable and egregious partiality to confine our view entirely to that principle by which our own minds operate." We know from experience the effects of these principles, but it is "no less intelligible or less conformable to experience to say that the world arose by vegetation, from a seed shed by another world, than to say that it arose from a divine reason or contrivance." (46).

6.2 Question-begging Theories

Demea attempts another tactic. He argues that if the world originated from plants or animals, this could happen only if they were designed to do so by an intelligent author. "From whence could arise so wonderful a faculty but from design?"

The answer to this is obvious. "To say that all this order in animals and vegetables proceeds ultimately from design is begging the question." (47) Demea has assumed the very thing he wants to prove, namely that the cause of the order we find in anything in the universe must arise ultimately from design.

Begging the question is a fallacy in which the author of an argument wrongly assumes that a relevant question has already received an affirmative answer. If I ask you "Why did you steal candy from the grocery store?" I am assuming (begging) an affirmative answer to the question "Did you steal candy from the grocery store?"

The question begged by Demea is "What is the origin of all the order we find in the universe?" Demea assumes that the correct answer is: "Reason and intelligence." If this answer is correct, then of course it follows that the order we find in animals and vegetables is the result of reason and intelligence. But Demea has yet to prove that this answer is correct.

How do we find the correct answer? Philo says "[Only by] experience and observation." (47) It is undeniable that vegetation and generation are experienced to be principles of order in nature. It is also undeniable that reason is a principle of order. Which principle should we choose? "The matter seems entirely arbitrary." (47)

Philo asks that we consider the consequences on both sides of this debate.

> *The world, I say, resembles an animal; therefore it is an animal, therefore it arose from generation. The steps, I confess are wide; yet there is some small appearance of analogy in each step. The world, says Cleanthes, resembles a machine; therefore it is a machine, therefore it arose from design. The steps are here equally wide, and the analogy less striking.* (47)

Cleanthes might attempt "to infer design or reason from the great principle of generation on which I insist," but Philo says that he can respond by pushing further Cleanthes' hypothesis, "and infer a divine generation or theogony from his principle of reason." Indeed, there is some foundation in experience for the latter inference. "Reason, in innumerable instances, is observed to arise from the principle of generation, and never to arise from any other principle." (48) We find reason only in animals, and we observe that humans are created (originate) through generation (procreation), not through vegetation, instinct, nor indeed, through reason itself (that is, we have never observed a human created from a plan or design).

Perhaps Hesiod "and all the ancient mythologists" were on firmer ground than the theists when they "universally explained the origin of nature from an animal birth and copulation." (48)

CHAPTER SEVEN

7. DEMEA'S *A PRIORI* ARGUMENT

(*Dialogues*, Part IX)

After witnessing Philo's complete destruction of Cleanthes' argument a posteriori for the nature of God (the Design Argument), Demea finally gets the opportunity to present his favorite a priori argument for both the existence and nature of God. He says that his argument is an "infallible demonstration," not an experimental argument which promises only a degree of probability to its conclusion. In contemporary terms, Demea's argument is deductive not inductive, thereby having a conclusion that the author claims to follow with certainty from its premises.

7.1 Necessary Existence

Here is a formal statement of Demea's argument, with commentary.

1. "Whatever exists must have a cause or reason for its existence, it being absolutely impossible for anything to produce itself or be the cause of its own existence" (54)

Demea does not defend this premise. He assumes that it is true a priori. A thing Q cannot be the cause of its own existence because this would imply that Q is both cause and effect, that is, Q would exist before Q exists, a logical impossibility.

---

2. If a thing Q cannot be the cause of itself, then Q must be the effect of a cause P, which immediately precedes Q and determines Q to exist by P's "power and efficacy."

3. "In mounting up from effects to causes, we must either (a) go on in tracing an infinite succession, without any ultimate cause at all, or we must (b) at last have recourse to some ultimate cause that is necessarily existent."

4. The first supposition (a) in (3) is absurd. The chain of causes and effects cannot be infinitely long, without an ultimate cause.

5. Therefore, the second supposition (b) in (3) is true, that is, there must be "some ultimate cause that is necessarily existent."

The key premise in Demea's argument is (4). Why is it "absurd" to claim that the whole eternal chain or succession of causes and effects, taken together, "is not determined or caused by anything"? Demea's reply is to devise a four-part disjunction. Our choices are determined either by external causes, by chance, by nothing, or by a "necessarily existent being" (55). He quickly eliminates the first three explanations.

> *External causes, there are supposed to be none. Chance is a word without a meaning. Was it nothing? But that can never produce anything.*

This leaves us with the fourth option:

> *We must, therefore, have recourse to a necessarily existent Being. who carries the reason of his existence in himself; and who cannot be supposed not to exist without an express contradiction.* (55)

7.2 The Impossibility of Demonstrating Matters of Fact

Cleanthes says that he will "point out the weakness of this metaphysical reasoning." (55) He begins by making this general observation: "[T]here is an evident absurdity in pretending to demonstrate a matter of fact, or to prove it by any arguments a priori." (55)

Hume elsewhere makes a distinction between matters of fact and relations of ideas (*Enquiry*, section IV). When we say that a triangle is a 3-sided shape, I am relating the idea (concept) of a triangle to the idea of a 3-sided shape. The relation is one of necessity. Triangles are necessarily three-sided shapes. But when I say that twentieth-century houses have indoor plumbing, I am not relating the idea of indoor plumbing to the idea of a house. I am not claiming that houses necessarily have indoor plumbing. I am asserting that this is a matter of fact, confirmable by observation, not by an analysis of ideas.

A demonstration or argument a priori is a deductive argument in which the conclusion is claimed to follow from the premises with certainty. Thus, one can demonstrate that "Socrates is mortal" by deducing this proposition as a conclusion drawn from the premises "Socrates is a man" and "All men are mortal." (Hume, *Enquiry*, id.). Notice, however, that this does not prove as a matter of fact that Socrates is mortal. Instead, we have proved only the hypothetical proposition "If Socrates is a man and all men are mortal, then Socrates is mortal." We might as well have said "If Socrates is a toad and all toads are Oxford graduates, then Socrates is an Oxford graduate."

7.3 Cleanthes' Rebuttal

Here is Cleanthes' step-by-step argument proving that the existence of God is not demonstrable.

1. Nothing is demonstrable unless the contrary implies a contradiction.

For example, "Bachelors are unmarried males" is demonstrable because the contrary ("Bachelors are married") implies a contradiction ("Unmarried males are married"). The proposition "All bachelors are less than 15 feet tall" although probably true, is not demonstrable because the contrary ("Some bachelors are more than 15 feet tall") does not contain a contradiction.

In sum, a proposition is demonstrable only if its negation implies a contradiction.

---

2. Nothing that is distinctly conceivable implies a contradiction.

It is conceivable that 15-foot-tall bachelors exist, as well as gremlins, trolls, elves and Santa Claus because it is not a contradiction to assert that any of these beings exist.

---

3. Whatever we conceive as existent, we can also conceive as nonexistent.

For example, we can conceive the existence of griffins and centaurs, but we cannot conceive the existence of two-sided triangles. We are "under a necessity" of conceiving triangles only as shapes having three-sides.

4. Therefore, there is no being whose non-existence implies a contradiction.

5. Therefore, there is no being whose existence is demonstrable.

6. The proposition "God does not exist" does not imply a contradiction.

7. Therefore, the existence of God is not demonstrable.

Cleanthes gives this summary of the argument:

It is pretended that the Deity is a necessarily existent being; and this necessity of his existence is attempted to be explained by asserting that, if we knew his whole essence or nature, we should perceive it to be as impossible for him not to exist, as for twice two not to be four. But it is evident that this can never happen while our faculties remain the same as at present. It will still be possible for us, at any time, to conceive the nonexistence of what we formerly conceived to exist; nor can the mind ever lie under a necessity of supposing any object to remain always in being; in the same manner as we lie under a necessity of always conceiving twice two to be four. The words, therefore, "necessary existence" have, no meaning or, which is the same thing, none that is consistent. (55-56)

Cleanthes' conclusion that the words "necessary existence" have no consistent meaning applies as well to the Ontological Argument for the Existence of God. Here is the standard version:

1. I have an idea (concept) of a supremely perfect being, that is, a being having all perfections.

2. Necessary existence is a perfection.

3. Therefore, a supremely perfect being exists.

Cleanthes concludes his demolition of the argument a priori for the existence of God with a reductio ad absurdum. He asks Demea, "why," instead of God, "may not the material universe be the necessarily existent being?" (56) If we insist that the necessity of God's existence is to be found in "his whole essence or nature," of which we are currently ignorant, then the same thing can be said of matter. "It may contain some qualities which, were they known, would make its non-existence appear as great a contradiction as that twice two is five."

This is a reductio ad absurdum response because it implies a conclusion (the material universe is necessarily existent) that Demea would not want to embrace.

Finally, Cleanthes goes after premise (4) of Demea's argument ("The chain of causes and effects cannot be infinitely long"). Cleanthes asks, "How can anything that exists from eternity have a cause, since that relation implies a priority in time and a beginning of existence." (56) That is, an infinite chain of causes and effects by definition would not have a first cause or a final effect. To insist that the chain must have a first cause or a final effect is to make the contradictory assumption that an infinite chain is finite.

Nor will it do to assert that "the whole chain wants a cause." Cleanthes answers that...

> *...the uniting of these parts into a whole, like the uniting of several distinct members into one body, is performed merely by an arbitrary act of the mind, and has no influence on the nature of things... [The cause of the whole body] "is sufficiently explained in explaining the cause of the parts"* (56).

If you unite several individuals into the same family because of shared DNA, this does not create a new entity that exists apart from the individuals that comprise the family. After you have been introduced to all of the individual members of the Smith family, you would not ask "But where is the Smith family? I would like to meet it." By analogy, after we have discovered a chain of causes and effects, there is no further entity called "*the chain* of causes and effects" which requires its own explanation.

CHAPTER EIGHT

8. THE PROBLEM OF EVIL

(*Dialogues*, Part X)

The theistic idea of God is that of "a supremely good being, creator of but separate from and independent of the world, omnipotent, omniscient, eternal, and self-existent" (Rowe, 2). It is this definition that presents one of the greatest challenges for those who believe in the existence of God.

8.1 Examples of Evil in the World

The existence of evil in the world is proclaimed by all three of the main characters in the dialogue. Philo says that "in all letters, sacred and profane, the topic of human misery has been insisted on with the most pathetic eloquence that sorrow and melancholy could inspire." (59) Demea agrees, responding that

> *The whole earth...is cursed and polluted. A perpetual war is kindled amongst all living creatures. Necessity, hunger, want stimulate the strong and courageous: fear, anxiety, terror agitate the weak and infirm. The first entrance into life gives anguish to the new-born infant and to its wretched parent: weakness, impotence, distress attend each stage of that life, and it is, at least, finished in agony and horror.* (59)

Demea joins in by adding the grim observation that much of the misery in the world is man-made:

> *Man is the greatest enemy of man. Oppression, injustice, contempt, contumely, violence, sedition, war, calumny, treachery, fraud; by these they mutually torment each other, and they would soon dissolve that society which they had formed were it not for the dread of still greater ills which must attend their separation.* (60)

He concludes with a dark description of the current human condition:

> *Were a stranger to drop on a sudden into this world, I would show him, as a specimen of its ills, a hospital full of diseases, a prison crowded with malefactors and debtors, a field of battle strewed with carcasses, a fleet foundering in the ocean, a nation languishing under tyranny, famine, or pestilence.* (61)

8.2 The Logical Problem of Evil

At this point, Philo changes the subject. He poses the logical problem of evil that has dogged theists for centuries:

> *And is it possible, Cleanthes, that...you can still persevere in your anthropomorphism, and assert the moral attributes of the Deity, his justice, benevolence, mercy and rectitude, to be of the same nature with these virtues in human creatures? His power, we allow, is infinite; whatever he wills is executed. But neither man nor any other animal is happy; therefore, he does not will their happiness. His wisdom is infinite; He is never mistaken in choosing the means to any end. But the course of nature tends not to human or animal felicity: Therefore, it is not established for that purpose...*

Philo concludes with these three questions:

> *Is [God] willing to prevent evil, but not able? Then he is impotent. Is he able, but not willing? Then he is malevolent. Is he both able and willing? Whence then is evil?* (63)

And we can add our own question: *Is God able and willing to prevent evil, but not aware of it? Then he is not omniscient.* The point of all this is that the perfections which believers attribute to God are logically inconsistent. We cannot consistently maintain the existence of a being who is omnipotent, omniscient and all-good. If evil exists, then one of these attributes must be discarded. If discarded, then we no longer have a perfect being.

8.3 Grasping at Straws

Cleanthes' first response is to agree with Philo. He goes even further by remarking "If you can make out the present point, and prove mankind to be unhappy or corrupted, there is an end at once of all religion" (64). Religion requires a god with moral attributes, "a god who is morally concerned with the world" (Gaskin, 42). If the world this god has ostensibly created is a world of human misery, then this has significant implications for the kind of god there could be. It would certainly not be the god of traditional theism.

Demea believes he can come to the rescue with a theory that the evil we see around us is "rectified in other regions, and in some future period or existence." Once we have this "larger view of things," and see the "whole connection of general laws," we will understand the necessity of contemporaneous human misery and how it is perfectly consistent with "the benevolence and rectitude of the Deity" (64).

Cleanthes immediately objects. He accuses Demea of grasping at straws when he offers a hypothesis that cannot be proved from the apparent phenomena. No cause can be known except from its known effects (64). Human misery is a known effect, but this does not tell us that it is caused by some event that occurs in a future period of existence. This is a conjecture which is possible, but one whose reality cannot be established.

Cleanthes takes a different approach by denying "absolutely the misery and wickedness of man." He says that fact and experience show that "health is more common than sickness: Pleasure than pain: Happiness than misery. And for one vexation which we meet with, we attain, upon computation, a hundred enjoyments." (65).

The obvious reply to Cleanthes is that his estimate of the amount of health over sickness, etc. is simply irrelevant. By saying that health is more common than sickness he is admitting that the evil of sickness exists. By saying that happiness is more common than misery, he is admitting that misery exists. To which Philo adds

> *"Why is there any misery at all in the world? Not by chance, surely. From some cause then. Is it from the intention of the Deity? But he is perfectly benevolent. Is it contrary to his intention? But he is almighty."* (66)

Philo concludes this part of the discussion with the remark that given the miserable condition of much of human life brought on by natural evil (floods, hurricane, earthquakes, disease) and moral evil (murder, rape, assault, the Holocaust), it is logically impossible to infer the existence of an infinitely benevolent, wise and powerful god.

CHAPTER NINE

9. THE FINITELY PERFECT DEITY

(*Dialogues*, Part XI)

Cleanthes asks Philo to take a new approach to his critique of the Design Argument. Let us drop the idea of infinite perfection. If we wish to use the analogical argument in which natural and moral evil is the effect, then any attempt to "reconcile any mixture of evil in the universe with infinite attributes" will always fail. Instead, let us suppose that "the Author of Nature" is "finitely perfect, though far exceeding mankind." Could we not then give a satisfactory account of the existence of natural and moral evil?

> *A lesser evil may then be chosen in order to avoid a greater; inconveniences may be submitted to in order to reach a desirable end; and, in a word, benevolence, regulated by wisdom and limited by necessity may produce just such a world as the present.* (67)

9.1 Two Scenarios

Philo responds to Cleanthes' request by imagining two scenarios. In the first, he supposes that a person of limited intelligence is utterly unacquainted with the universe but is assured that it is "the production of a very good, wise and powerful being." In the second scenario, "which is the real case with regard to man," the imaginary person has no beliefs about who or what created the universe, "but is left to gather such a belief from the appearances of things" (68-69)

In the first scenario, Philo says that once this person finds out about the degree of human misery in the world, although he would be surprised and disappointed, he would probably not alter his belief about the attributes of the god who he believes is the creator of this world.

> *Such a limited intelligence must be sensible of his own blindness and ignorance, and must allow that there may be many solutions of these phenomena which will forever escape his comprehension.*

In the second scenario, the person would never find a reason for concluding that the evil (misery) he has witnessed is proof of a supreme intelligence, benevolent and powerful. He would form an inference "from what he knows, not from what he is ignorant of." (68)

Philo invents an example to prove his point. Suppose that you were shown a house "where there was not one [room] convenient or agreeable; where the windows, doors, fires, passages, stairs, and the whole economy of the building were the source of noise, confusion, fatigue, darkness, and the extremes of heat and cold." Surely you would blame these ill effects on the house itself, and ultimately put the blame on the architect.

And even if the architect convinced you that one or two adjustments would make the house even worse, you would assert in general that,

> *If the architect had had skill and good intentions, he might have formed such a plan of the whole, and might have adjusted the parts in such a manner as would have remedied all or most of these inconveniences... If you find any inconveniences and deformities in the building, you will always, without entering into any detail, condemn the architect* (68-69).

Philo's point is that the world, "as it appears to us in this life" has effects that are analogous to the effects of the poorly constructed house. The world is quite different from what a person would, beforehand, expect from a very powerful, wise and benevolent deity. The human misery this person observes can be traced to poor design. The fact that there is a kind of adjustment of parts in the world (as there is an adjustment in the parts of the imagined deformed house) is not relevant. Hence, the mere "working together" of these parts "can never afford us an inference concerning the existence of a finitely perfect Deity" (69)

9.2 There are no Unavoidable Evils

Philo now extends his argument by positing that there are four circumstances causing misery to humans and other "sensible creatures" and none of these circumstances are "in the least degree necessary or unavoidable" (69). Philo's conclusion in the following discussion is that each circumstance is such that it could have been prevented by a finitely perfect Deity.

The first circumstance is the pain which "excites all creatures to action" for the purpose of self-preservation. Surely, it may be argued, it is necessary that all creatures feel pain in order to be alerted to threats on their life. Philo's reply is that this is not necessary. "Pleasure alone...is sufficient for this purpose." (69) A benevolent deity might have constructed animals in such a way that they are "constantly in a state of enjoyment." When they are thirsty or hungry, what they feel is not pain but "a diminution of pleasure," which is sufficient to motivate them to drink or eat. "It seems, therefore, plainly possible to carry on the business of life without any pain" (69-70).

The second circumstance said to be unavoidable to a finitely powerful, wise and benevolent Deity is the "conducting of the world by general laws" (70). If he undetectably intervened every time there is a threat to human life or well-being, then "the course of nature would be perpetually broken and no man could employ his reason in the conduct of life." Humans and other animals would not have to take care when acting in ways that might lead to their death or serious injury because "all serious hazards would be obviated by a complex system of avoidance or transformation..." (Hick, 341). But even if "exact sciences could not be formulated" in such a bizarre world, this does not imply that it would be worse.

> *The Deity [could] exterminate all ill, wherever it [is] to be found, and produce all good, without any preparation or long progress of causes and effects" (70).*

Philo's reply is that all incidents which we now call "accidents" or "chance" could be turned to the good of mankind by a powerful deity who knows "the secret springs of the universe" and wants to "render the whole world happy, without discovering himself in any operation" (7) To paraphrase Philo's suggestion about the cruel Roman emperor Caligula, we can imagine a scenario in which a few small touches given to Hitler's brain in his infancy would have converted him into a benevolent leader of Germany who would never have conceived the Holocaust or launch World War II.

The third circumstance causing misery to humans and other animals is "the great frugality with which all powers and faculties are distributed to every particular being" (71). The human species, Philo says, "whose chief excellence is reason and sagacity, is of all others the most necessitous, and the most deficient in bodily advantage." They do not have "the wings of the eagle, the swiftness of the stag, the force of the ox, the arms of the lion, or the scales of the crocodile or rhinoceros." Perhaps of more importance, is the low propensity of humans to industry and labor, otherwise known as "idleness." There is no reason why a finitely perfect Author of Nature could not correct this deficiency. It could be done in a way that would give all persons "naturally an equal diligence" and thereby reap considerable benefits.

> *Almost all the moral as well as natural evils of human life arise from idleness; and were our species, by the original constitu-*

> *tion of their frame, exempt from this vice or infirmity, the perfect cultivation of land, the improvement of arts and manufactures, the exact execution of every office and duty, immediately follow; and men at once may fully reach that state of society which is so imperfectly attained by the best regulated government (72).*

The fourth and final candidate for a circumstance that might produce "misery and ill of the universe" and which (it is claimed) could be prevented by a finite deity is "the inaccurate workmanship of all the springs and principles of the great machine of nature" (73).

> *Thus, the winds are requisite to convey the vapors along the surface of the globe, and to assist men in navigation: But how often, rising up to tempests and hurricanes, do they become pernicious? Rains are necessary to nourish all the plants and animals of the earth: But how often are they defective? How often excessive? Heat is requisite to all life and vegetation but is not always found in the due proportion. On the mixture and secretion of the humors and juices of the body depend the health and prosperity of the animal: But the parts perform not regularly their function. What more useful than all the passions of the mind, ambition, vanity, love, anger? But how often do they break their bounds and cause the greatest convulsion in society? (73)*

This completes Philo's lengthy account of the four circumstances on which together "the greatest part of natural evil" depends (73). If these circumstances were either eliminated or prevented (by particular acts of a finitely perfect Deity), "evil could never have found access into the universe" (73). Now if we do not assume the finite goodness of the Deity but try to infer this attribute from what we witness, we would fail to make the inference. "[T]here can be no grounds for such an inference while there are so many ills in the universe, ...while these ills might so easily have been remedied..." (74).

What Philo has said about natural evil applies to moral evil as well:

> *We have no more reason to infer that the rectitude of the Supreme Being resembles human rectitude than that his benevolence resembles the human. Nay it will be thought that we have still greater cause to exclude from him moral sentiments, such as we feel them; since moral evil, in the opinion of many, is much more predominant above moral good than natural evil above natural good. (75)*

9.3 Demea's Angry Departure

Demea is once again outraged by Philo's reasoning. He feels betrayed. He thought that Philo was going to join with him in proving "the incomprehensible nature of the Divine Being," by refuting the attempts of Cleanthes to use analogical reasoning to prove the human-like attributes of the Deity. Instead, Philo has gone too far. He has proved that a benevolent god cannot be inferred from what we observe about the world and its human inhabitants. If it is assumed that the Deity is both (finitely) benevolent and (finitely) omnipotent, then the facts about natural and moral evil make it highly probable that such a being does not exist. We must give up either the idea that God is very good or that God is very powerful. But if we give up either of these attributes, then we are giving up the idea that god exists. And with this realization, Demea, "on some pretense or other," walks out.

CHAPTER TEN

10. CONFESSION AND CONFUSION

(*Dialogues*, Part XII)

After the abrupt departure of Demea, Cleanthes and Philo continue the conversation. It is here that Hume astounds readers of the *Dialogues* by having the sceptic Philo "confess" to the following:

> *A purpose, an intention, a design strikes everywhere the most careless, stupid thinker; and no man can be so hardened in absurd systems as at all times to reject it.* (77)

Philo goes on to say:

> *If there was a God who did not discover himself immediately to our senses, [he could not] give stronger proofs of his existence than what appears on the whole face of nature* (78).

Moreover, Philo continues, what appears in nature is "order and design." Seeing an opening, Cleanthes now repeats his original claim (apparently ignoring the critique in the previous lengthy discussion):

> *...the comparison of the universe to a machine of human contrivance is so obvious and natural, and is justified by so many instances of order and design in nature, that it must immediately strike all unprejudiced apprehensions and procure universal approbation.* (79)

Philo further astounds us by accepting Cleanthes' comparison! He then compounds our confusion with the claim that "sound reason," allows the inference that God exists:

> ...according to all the rules of good reasoning, we ought to infer, if we argue at all concerning them, that the causes [of a machine and of the universe] have a proportional analogy. But as there are also considerable differences, we have reason to suppose a proportional difference in the cause, and, in particular ought to attribute a much higher degree of power and energy to the Supreme Cause than any we have ever observed in mankind. Here, then, the existence of a Deity is plainly... ascertained by reason (79).

If there are those who insist that "Mind" or "Thought" bear a better resemblance to the human mind than "God" or "Deity," then Philo will allow them to use these words to refer to the Supreme Cause. However, he believes that the choice of terms is a "mere verbal" matter. All of these words refer to one and the same thing.

What are we to say about Philo's about face? Philo had earlier maintained that "we cannot infer the existence of an infinitely benevolent, wise and powerful god" from the fact of evil in the world (Ch. 8, *supra*.). And if there is a limit to god's benevolence, wisdom and power, then we must infer that this less-than-perfect god either does not know about the evil, does not have the power to prevent it, or simply does not care. But when asked here about the consequence of inferring that "the natural attributes of the Deity have a greater resemblance to those of men than his moral have to human virtues," Philo responds:

> Nothing but this, that the moral qualities of man are more defective in their kind than his natural abilities. For as the Supreme Being is allowed to be absolutely and entirely perfect, whatever differs most from him departs the farthest from the supreme standard of rectitude and perfection (81).

In other words, the Deity/Mind sets the standard for moral virtue, but what actually happens in the world (oppression, injustice, violence, etc.) has no relevance to what we can say about the moral attributes of the Deity/Mind.

> *There is no view of human life or of the condition of mankind from which, without the greatest violence, we can infer the moral attributes or learn that infinite benevolence, conjoined with infinite power and infinite wisdom, which we must discover by the eyes of faith alone* (66).

If he had not walked out, Demea would be pleased by this shift from a posteriori to a priori reasoning. Demea had said that God is "infinitely perfect" (14), and because we know this a priori, no amount of empirical data about the evil behavior of human beings could alter God's infinite benevolence.

The reader has every right to be confused by Part XII of the *Dialogue* (Ch. 10, supra). Philo's final statement about the Argument from Design is that "the most inquisitive, contemplative and religious man" can reasonably give assent to the proposition "That the cause or causes of order in the universe probably bear remote analogy to human intelligence" (88). Of course he can assent to this. But Philo has also said previously in Part VII (Ch. 6, supra) that "the world plainly resembles more an animal or a vegetable than it does a watch or a knitting-loom." It follows that "it is more probable" that the origin of the universe "ought rather to be ascribed to generation or vegetation than to reason and design" (44). However, even though this is more probable, it does not imply high probability, for it is only a remote analogy. We can safely assume that the resemblance of the universe to a watch or a knitting loom is also remote, albeit less remote.

The final words of the *Dialogues* are uttered by Pamphilus, who has audited and recited the entire discussion: "Upon a serious review of the whole, I cannot but think that Philo's principles are more probable than Demea's, but those of Cleanthes approach still nearer to the truth" (89).

Cleanthes principle is empirical, using a posteriori analogical reasoning. Philo's principles place limits on what we can learn from experience and analogies: "Our ideas reach no farther than our experience," and "Like effects prove like causes." Demea's approach is to use only the "simple and sublime argument a priori."

Why does Hume have Pamphilus say that Cleanthes principles are nearer to the truth? It may be because this is consistent with Philo's apparent concession that, despite his constant barrage of criticisms of the argument from design, there is a "remote analogy" of the universe to a machine and from this analogy we can infer that the universe is the product of an intelligent designer. But this explanation begs the question "Why does Hume have Philo concede?"

On this last question, there has been considerable debate, but it is a debate that is personal and political, not philosophical. Some have said that Part XII is Hume's way of showing his Christian readers that he is not, after all a raging atheist. Others have said that since Philo has clearly won the debate by the end of Part XI, he is giving an olive branch to Cleanthes as a conciliatory gesture. For my part, further discussion of this non-philosophical topic is beyond the bounds of this inquiry. I invite you to see the references and bibliography at the end of this book if you wish to pursue further the mystery of Part XI.

CHAPTER ELEVEN

11. POSTSCRIPT: A HUMEAN RESPONSE TO THE INTELLIGENT DESIGN ARGUMENT

Hume's skepticism about the Argument from Design did not spell the end of attempts to prove that our world and the universe itself are the product of an intelligent designer. In the twentieth and twenty-first century there have been several efforts to resurrect the argument. Under the heading "Intelligent Design," some philosophers, physicists and religious persons begin their argument not with an analogy between the universe and human-made machines, but with the mathematically small chance ("much less than one chance in a million") that the universe developed in such a way that life is possible. They conclude from this that "the hypothesis of an intelligent/designer who fine-tuned the initial state of the universe seems a much more likely explanation of the fact that our universe is suitable for life than an appeal to mere chance" (Rowe, 46).

Let us assume as fact two hypotheses (theories) about the origin of the universe that were unknown to David Hume. The first assumption is the Big Bang theory. "At its simplest, it says the universe as we know it started with a small singularity, then inflated over the next 13.8 billion years to the cosmos that we know today" (Howell). The second assumption is Stephen Hawking's estimate about the rate of expansion of the universe from the singularity: "If the rate of expansion one second after the 'big bang' had been smaller by even one part in a hundred thousand million million, the universe would have recollapsed into a hot fireball" (123).

Using these facts as background, here is the new Intelligent Design Argument for the conclusion that an intelligent being intervened to design and create our universe.

1. Either the initial conditions of the universe were the product of natural forces or they were the product of the intervention of an intelligent being.

2 If the initial conditions of the universe led to the existence of life as we know it, then it is highly improbable that these conditions were mere chance (that is, the product of natural forces).

3. The initial conditions of the universe did lead to the existence of life as we now know it.

4. Therefore, it is highly improbable that the initial conditions of the universe were the product of mere chance (natural forces). [from premises 2 and 3]

5. Therefore, the initial conditions of the universe were the product of the intervention of an intelligent designer. [from premises 1 and 4]

The first thing we should note is that this is an argument a posteriori. It leads to the probability not the certainty of the conclusion. Perhaps (5) would be best stated as:

(5a) It is more likely that the initial conditions of the universe were the product of an intervention of an intelligent designer than that these conditions were the product of natural causes.

What would Hume say about this argument if he had had the opportunity to think about it? The first thing he would ask is "What support is there for premise (2)?" How are we to know that a universe that is suitable for life is much more likely to be caused by an intelligent designer than by natural forces? This is where Hume's principles are relevant. All conclusions concerning matters of fact that should be tested by their adherence to two principles: (a) All inferences concerning fact must be founded on experience; and (b) the experimental principle that only like effects prove like causes and vice versa.

As to (a), no one has yet experienced the origin of a universe. Hume mentions several possible natural forces besides intelligence. But without confirmable and testable observations of the creation of universes, it is a symptom of human bias and hubris that philosophers continue to select intelligence "as the original cause of all things" (19). Hume mentions vegetation and generation as natural forces of change. In contemporary science, the forces of nature include gravitation, electromagnetism, and the strong and weak nuclear forces. Intelligence has no more claim to be the cause of the universe as we know it than does any of the aforementioned natural forces.

If no one has had an experience or observation of universe design and construction, then (Hume argues) we must turn to the experimental principle (b) and look for relevant analogies. A popular contemporary analogy begins with a thought experiment in which 347 black and white beads are thrown on the floor. There is very little chance that the beads will land in such a way that they form a full sentence, (e.g. the sentence "David Hume died in 1776.") "If there are 347 beads, the statistical chance that they should appear in any specific sequence is ...about 3×10 to the 104th, a 10 with 104 zeroes after it" (Missler, 2). If you walk into a room and find 347 beads arranged in such a way that they form an understandable English sentence, then your first thought would be "Who wrote this?" not "What force of nature caused this?" Your past experience of order and language has taught you that an intelligent being must have been the source of the words formed by the beads on the floor.

This is the kind of analogy used to support premise (2) above. If it is highly unlikely that natural forces explain how the beads thrown on the floor landed in such a way as to form an understandable sentence, then it should also be highly unlikely that natural forces would be our "go to" explanation for the existence of life in the universe. As Hawking's data implies, the chances of the latter event happening are infinitesimal.

"Like effects prove like causes." The relevant effects are "Life as we know it" and "An understandable sentence made up out of beads". The alleged cause in both cases is "an intelligent designer." Now it is assumed by proponents of the Intelligent Design Argument that there is a resemblance between the things we have experienced to be caused by intelligent design (e.g. sentences written on paper in ink or on the floor in beads) and all universes that have and support life. But what is this resemblance or likeness? When we look at a sentence with its words made out of beads, we see order and language. But when we look at the life we see around us, it is not clear how this resembles an understandable English sentence any more than it resembles a kitchen sink. Hume would argue that since the effects have little or no resemblance to one another, then the causes must also bear little or no resemblance. That is, we have no good reason to think that the presence of life in our universe has the same cause as an understandable sentence composed of beads.

It may be objected that we have got our analogies wrong. The analogy is not between understandable English sentences and life supporting universes *per se*. It is between the chance that the former and the latter are both the consequence of natural forces, as compared to the chance that both are the consequence of an intelligent designer. Since the chance is very small that the understandable English sentence is the consequence of natural forces, then we should conclude the same for life supporting universes.

But this objection begs the question "Why are the chances of the one the same as the chances of the other?" We know from experience that the chance of the English sentence being the product of natural forces is minimal. But this tells us nothing about the chance that a life supporting universe was caused by natural forces. In fact, it tells us nothing about the cause of any kind of universe, whether it is a universe that supports life or it is a universe that does not support life. If a universe that provides the conditions for the support of life as we know it is said to be evidence of an intelligent designer, then so is every other possible universe that could have come about as the result of the Big Bang. Whether or not a possible universe has conditions supporting life, a case can be made that the chance of its very existence was one of a "hundred thousand million million." It is not the fact that a universe provides the conditions for the support of life that makes it eligible for the honorific title of being created by an intelligent designer, but the slight probability that life exists at all. Since each possible universe has only a slight chance of coming into existence at the time of the Big Bang, we are forced to conclude that all of them must be the product of intelligent design. And the same can be said of Hawking's imagined "fire ball" event: God did it!

Questions for thought and discussion

1. In chapter 2 (supra), Philo says that the perfections of God do not "have any resemblance to these qualities among men. He is infinitely superior to our limited view and comprehension." If all of our ideas about matters of fact originate in experience, then how is it possible to have an idea of God's perfection?

2. Explain the Argument from Design. Why is it classified as an analogical argument? Why is it also classified as a posteriori (inductive) rather than a priori (deductive)?

3. In his criticism of the Argument from Design, Philo challenges Cleanthes to answer the questions "What is the purpose or end of the universe?" and "How do the parts of the universe serve this purpose?" Does Cleanthes give satisfactory answers to these questions? How would you answer them?

4. How does Cleanthes' analogy between human legs and the steps of a stair (2.3 supra) advance his argument that the universe is (likely) the product of intelligent design?

5. In your own words, what point is Philo trying to make about the nature of God when he asks Demea "to contemplate your ideas (concepts), abstracted from everything you know or have ever seen"? (2.5.1 supra)

6. How does Philo argue for the claim that the experimental argument for the nature of the Deity gives more support to the polytheistic religion of the ancient Greeks with its finite and imperfect gods than it does to the theistic Abrahamic religions with its one infinite and perfect God? (5.7 supra). Do you agree? Explain.

7. The philosopher Nietzsche famously proclaimed, "God is dead!" Can this be proved or disproved by the Argument from Design?

8. Do Philo and Demea give an adequate response to the challenge of Cleanthes' two thought experiments (voice in the clouds and books growing on trees) in Chapter 3 (supra)?

9. What is the problem of evil? Can the Argument from Design be used to solve it? Does it advance Cleanthes' argument to switch from consideration of God as an infinite being to God as a finite being? Explain.

10. Explain Demea's a priori argument for the existence and nature of God.

11. Why does Cleanthes say that there is "an evident absurdity in pretending to demonstrate a matter of fact, or to prove it by any arguments a priori"?

12. Do you agree with the assessment of Pamphilus (the interlocutor) that although "Philo's principles are more probable than Demea's, ... those of Cleanthes approach still nearer to the truth"? How do the principles of Cleanthes differ from those of Philo?

13. What can we conclude about the attributes of the "intelligent designer" from the Intelligent Design argument discussed in the postscript (chapter 10)?

References

Bartha, Paul, "Analogy and Analogical Reasoning", The Stanford Encyclopedia of Philosophy (Winter 2016 Edition), Edward N. Zalta (ed.), https://plato.stanford.edu/archives/win2016/entries/reasoning-analogy

Bele, Mchael J. 2003. "The Modern Design Hypothesis: Breaking Rules," in Manson, Neil A. ed. God and Design: The Teleological Argument and Modern Science. New York: Routledge.

Bennett, B. Logically Fallacious. 2019. https://www.logicallyfallacious.com/tools/lp/Bo/LogicalFallacies/151/Reductio-ad-Absurdum

Gaskin, J.C.A. 1978. Hume's Philosophy of Religion. London: Macmillan Press.

Hawking, Stephen. 1988. A Brief History of Time. New York: Bantam Books.

Howell, Elizabeth. 2017. "What is the Big Bang Theory?" Science and Astronomy. https://www.space.com/25126-big-bang-theory.html

Hume, David. 1977 [1748]. Inquiry Concerning Human Understanding. Steinberg, Eric (ed.). Indianapolis: Hackett.

Hurlbutt, Robert H., 1985. Hume, Newton and the Design Argument, revised edition, Lincoln & London: University of Nebraska Press.

Missler, Chuck. 2016. Beyond Coincidence. Coer d'Alene, Idaho: Koinonia House.

Morris, William Edward and Brown, Charlotte R., "David Hume", The Stanford Encyclopedia of Philosophy (Spring 2017 Edition), Edward N. Zalta (ed.),
https://plato.stanford.edu/archives/spr2017/entries/hume

Nietzsche, Friedrich. 1974 [1882]. Kaufman, W. (trans.), The Gay Science New York: Vintage Books (section 108).

Nolan, Lawrence, "Descartes' Ontological Argument", The Stanford Encyclopedia of Philosophy (Fall 2015 Edition), Edward N. Zalta (ed.), https://plato.stanford.edu/archives/fall2015/entries/descartes-ontological

O'Connor, David. 2001. Hume On Religion, London & New York: Routledge.

Phillips, D.Z., and Timothy Tessin. (eds.),1999, Religion and Hume's Legacy, London: Palgrave Macmillan.

Rowe, William L. 2007. Philosophy of Religion: An Introduction, 4th edition. Belmont, CA. Wadsworth.

Russell, Paul and Kraal, Anders, "Hume on Religion", The Stanford Encyclopedia of Philosophy (Summer 2017 Edition), Edward N. Zalta (ed.), https://plato.stanford.edu/archives/sum2017/entries/hume-religion

Smith, N.K., 1941. The Philosophy of David Hume, London: Macmillan

III   A GUIDE TO *OF MIRACLES*

CHAPTER TWELVE

12. DEFINITIONS AND STANDARDS

[The full text of Hume's *Of Miracles* is reprinted in Appendix A]

(*Of Miracles*, Part I)

There is a popular use of the word "miracle" in which we call an event a miracle if it is both surprising and welcome. For example, our favorite soccer (football) team scores the winning goal in the last seconds of the championship match, upsetting the heavily favored opponent. "It's a miracle!" we happily shout. But we do not mean by these words that the unexpected goal defied the laws of nature (science) or that the gods intervened to guide the ball into the net.

There is another use of the word "miracle" that does mean or imply that a law of nature has been violated and/or that there has been a divine intervention in the natural course of events. The context in which the word "miracle" is used in this way is often found in religion. For example, Christians refer to the resurrection of Jesus as a miracle, not only in the sense that they celebrate this as a welcome event, but in the larger sense that it defied the laws of nature. People do not climb out of burial caves or graves and walk the earth after death. If there has been cessation of all vital bodily functions (cerebral, respiratory and circulatory) for more than 30 minutes, then experience teaches us that these functions will permanently cease (Dorland Medical Dictionary). The dead will remain dead. If these vital functions are restored then we would refer to this reversal of death as a miracle. There is nothing in contemporary laws of medical science that would explain this event. If we ask for an explanation, then Christians would undoubtedly refer to the intervention of God.

In the essay "Of Miracles" (reprinted below in Part VIII, Appendix A), David Hume discusses miracles in the second (religious) sense of this term, but he does this in an unusual way. He focuses on the *witnesses* to an alleged miracle rather than on the miracle itself. Hume's first question is about the conditions under which a witness report is believable, whether or not said report is about a traffic accident or a resurrection. If he can answer this question about traffic accidents, then he will be in a better position to extract a plausible standard and apply it to resurrections and other religious miracles.

Hume attempts to prove that it is always more reasonable to believe that the witnesses to an alleged miracle are in error than it is to believe that a miracle actually occurred. In the process of accomplishing this goal, Hume shifts back and forth between two questions: "Is it probable that a miracle occurred?" and "Are the witnesses to the alleged miracle credible?"

Both questions are answered. This chapter (12) is about Hume's definition of "miracle" and the standard we should use to determine whether or not a miracle has occurred. Chapter 13 is about Hume's proof that the probability that what a witness says (about a miracle) is false is always much greater than the probability that it is true.

12.1 Direct Evidence

Hume begins his discussion by praising another scholar who had published an essay "against the real presence." The words "real presence" refer to "the Roman Catholic doctrine that the body and blood of Jesus Christ are really present in the bread and wine" taken during holy communion. Hume writes that the doctrine is "little worthy of serious refutation" because it is "directly contrary to the rules of just reasoning." These rules require direct evidence, such as the kind of evidence provided by observation and other forms of perception (auditory, olfactory, tactilely). But the bread and wine do not provide this. Instead, the person taking communion is told by the vicar or minister that the body and blood of Christ are in the bread and wine. This is merely "external evidence" that "contradicts sense." Despite what the priest tells the parishioners, not everyone feels "the immediate operation of the Holy Spirit" (107), nor can they infer his presence from the sensible acts of seeing, eating, tasting, and smelling the bread and the wine.

Hume uses this example as an introduction to his announcement that he has "discovered an argument of a like nature" which will serve as "an everlasting check to all kinds of superstitious delusion," including not only the Roman Catholic belief in the real presence, but also the nearly universal belief in "miracles and prodigies" (108).

In the 19th century the word "prodigy," meant an amazing or unusual thing or event, especially one out of the ordinary course of nature." For example, "Omens and prodigies abound in Livy's work" (Cambridge English dictionary).

12.2 Hume's Definition of "Miracle"

What is the argument that Hume thinks he has discovered? How does it serve as a "check" on the belief in miracles and prodigies? Hume answers these questions in several steps:

Hume defines a miracle as "a violation of the laws of nature" (111). In a later footnote Hume offers a "more accurate definition": A miracle is "a transgression of a law of nature by a particular volition of the Deity, or by the interposition of some invisible agent" (fn. 4). The implication of the longer definition is that an event that transgresses a law of nature would constitute a miracle only if the transgression was caused by the will of God or the will of an invisible agent. We will return to investigate this part of the definition in section 12.6.

12.3 Transgressions of the Law of Nature

Transgressing (violating) a law of nature is not like transgressing a moral or legal law. The latter laws prescribe (compel) human behavior. If I tell a lie or drive through a red light, I am liable to blame or punishment, and it is the blame or punishment that deters me from doing these things. But laws of nature are not prescriptive. They do not compel nor deter behavior. The planets that circle the sun do not stay in their orbits because they fear the consequences of disobeying Kepler's laws of planetary motion. Instead these laws (and all laws of science) describe past experience of the regularity (constancy) of the motion and this, in turn, allows accurate predictions about future motion. Hence, a transgression of Kepler's laws would only occur if there was "an opposition of experiments and observations" showing a contrariety of events. In that case, instead of saying that Kepler's laws had been violated, we would say that they had been disproved by the evidence, requiring a revision of the laws.

12.4 Proportioning Belief to the Evidence.

Here are Hume's words about "just" reasonings concerning matters of fact:

> *A wise man, therefore, proportions his belief to the evidence. In such conclusions as are founded on an infallible experience, he expects the event with the last degree of assurance, and regards his past experience as a full proof of the future existence of that event. In other cases he proceeds with more caution: He weighs the opposite experiments: He considers which side is supported by the greater number of experiments: To that side he inclines, with doubt and hesitation; and when at last he fixes*

his judgment, the evidence exceeds not what we properly call probability. All probability, then, supposes an opposition of experiments and observations, where the one side is found to overbalance the other, and to produce a degree of evidence, proportioned by to the superiority (108).

Kepler's laws of planetary motion are an example of what Hume means by a "full proof," in which a conclusion is founded on infallible evidence. The evidence is from observation and experience, summarized by Kepler in three mathematical formulas (see University of Nebraska, Astronomy Education). The formulas allow astronomers to make accurate predictions about planetary motion.

12.5 Fallible Reasoning Concerning Matters of Fact

All effects follow not with like certainty from their supposed causes (108).

By "like certainty" Hume means "same probability." In England, for example, you would expect better weather in May than in December and this would be a correct inference that conforms with your experience. But it may happen that you are mistaken about this and find yourself (as I once was) in the midst of a London snowstorm in May. You have no cause to complain about past experience. If you had looked closely and diligently you would have found the variables that sometimes bring about snow during the late springtime months. You would use this variability in making future predictions about London weather. Your predictions in most cases would amount to a high degree of probability that there will be better weather in May than in December.

12.6 Reasoning Based on Human Testimony

Reasonings based on human testimony, "and the reports of eyewitnesses and spectators" are a species of reasonings founded on the relation of cause and effect. If my wife tells me that the car keys I have been looking for are in my coat pocket, my assurance that the keys are in fact in my coat pocket is based on past experience of the veracity of her testimony. And in general, we are inclined to accept human testimony as correct because of "the usual conformity of facts to the reports of witnesses" testimony

> *It being a general maxim that no objects have any discoverable connection together, and that all the inferences, which we can draw from one to another, are founded merely on our experience of their constant and regular conjunction.*

I cannot infer that billiard ball B will move from location T1 to location T2 when struck by billiard ball A unless I have had prior experiences of the conjunction of events like this. I certainly cannot discover a causal connection between A and B by contemplating the concept of "billiard ball." The general maxim (above) applies to witness testimony as well: I am inclined to accept my wife's testimony about the location of my car keys because I know from past experience that her testimony is true.

The general maxim applies to the veracity of human testimony. If we have an experience of the constant and regular conjunction between the event of being told by another person that a proposition P is true and the truth of P, then I can draw an inference from the former to the latter, as in the case of being told by my wife that my car keys are in my coat pocket. But there is "no discoverable connection" between testimony and truth. That is, the proposition "She told me that my car keys are in my coat pocket" does not logically imply "The car keys are in my coat pocket" (she could be mistaken). The inference can be made only after many experiences of the "constant and regular conjunction" of the testimony and the veracity of the testimony.

> *And as the evidence, derived from witnesses and human, is founded on past experience, so it varies with the experience, and is regarded as a proof or a probability, according as the conjunction between any particular kind of report and any kind of object has been found to be constant or variable.*

12.7 Disputes About the Veracity of Human Testimony

Hume writes that "the ultimate standard" for settling disputes that may arise concerning the reports or testimony of others "comes from experience and observation." There are reasons why doubts might arise about these reports, each of which can be traced to prior experience.

> *Contrariety of evidence can arise from the opposition of contrary testimony; from the character or number of witnesses; from the manner of their delivering their testimony; or from the union of all these circumstances*

Contemporary examples can be drawn from science, from everyday life, and from politics. (a) A scientist recently announced that plasma infusions from young people provide benefits against normal aging, Alzheimer's disease, and a host of other diseases, but the federal Food and Drug Administration warned that there is "no proven clinical benefit" from the procedure (Robbins). (b)

Thousands of persons have reported sightings of unidentified flying objects (UFOs). Many persons believe that the UFOs are spacecraft from other worlds. However, most of the sightings were classified by the U.S. Air Force as (a) "identified" with a known astronomical, atmospheric, or artificial (human-caused) phenomenon or (b) "unidentified." The latter category, approximately 6 percent of the total, included cases for which there was insufficient information to make an identification with a known phenomenon (Shostak). (c) The U.S. president declares that there is "a crisis at the southern border," citing hordes of dangerous immigrants "invading" the United States from Mexico. The president's testimony is strongly rebutted by others who argue that most of the immigrants are seeking asylum from violence and poverty, not for opportunities to engage in criminal behavior.

12.8 Miracles and the Rules of Just Reasoning

None of the previous examples were regarded by advocates or the disputants as miraculous events. As stated earlier, Hume defines a miracle as "a violation of the laws of nature." Testimony about the benefits of plasma infusions, sightings of flying saucers, and hordes of illegal immigrants bent on criminal behavior are not about events that defy scientific law. "Nothing is a miracle if it ever happens in the common course of nature" (111). But what are we to say if a man who has been declared dead, has been buried for several months, and is now reported by several persons to have come back to life? Is this not a miracle? Hume's answer:

> *There must...be a uniform experience against every miraculous event – otherwise the event would not merit that appellation. And as a uniform experience amounts to a proof, there is here a direct and full proof from the nature of the fact, against the ex-*

istence of any miracle; nor can such a proof be destroyed, or the miracle rendered credible but by an opposite proof, which is superior.

For example, if a man in good health suddenly dies, that would not constitute a miracle because sudden death of healthy people (for example, by heart attack) is known to frequently happen. But if we hear reports about a long-dead man suddenly coming back to life, we would certainly be amazed and call this a miracle because such events have "never been observed, in any age or country." At the same time, all of the data we have from the past about death "amounts to a full proof, from the nature of the fact, against the existence of any miracle" (111). We would be justified in saying that the witnesses to this event are either deceiving us or have been deceived by others.

In a footnote, Hume gives an example of a man who appears to have the ability to "order many natural events, which immediately follow upon his command." This divine says the words "Get up and walk!" to a paraplegic and she rises from her chair and walks around the room. This is an example of "an event that would not have occurred had what transpired been due only to natural causes; the course of nature would not have produced the event" (Rowe, 153). The paraplegic would not have stood up, and the dead, decomposed man in the previous example would not have risen from the grave. The presence of natural causes is what prompts Hume to declare that a miracle is an event that would not have transpired had the event been due only to natural causes. Therefore, Hume writes, a miracle must be "a transgression of a law of nature by a particular violation of the Deity; or by the interposition of some invisible agent" (fn. 4). Despite the natural causes of her disability, the only explanation of the event of the paraplegic rising from her chair and walking across the room is the intervention of the Deity or some other "invisible agent." Hume is also quick to caution that he is only offering a definition of a miracle. He has yet to tell us whether it is reasonable to believe that a miracle has occurred.

In the final paragraph of Part I, Hume cites another general maxim:

> *No testimony is sufficient to establish a miracle unless the testimony be of such a kind, that its falsehood would be more miraculous, than the fact, which it endeavors to establish: And even in that case there is a mutual destruction of arguments, and the superior only gives us an assurance suitable to that degree of force, which remains, after deducting the inferior*

Suppose that someone tells us that she saw "a dead person restored to life" (we shall again assume that the body has been buried for several months). We should ask whether it is more probable that this alleged eye witness is mistaken than that this event actually took place. Would the falsehood of her testimony about the event be more miraculous than it being true that a dead person was restored to life? Although it is logically (but not physically) possible for a dead and decomposed person to come alive and rise from the grave, Hume argues that it is far more probable that the witness is lying or has been deceived by what she saw.

CHAPTER THIRTEEN

13. THE PROBABILITY OF MIRACLES

(*Of Miracles*, Part II)

Although miracles are logically possible, Hume argues that "there never was a miraculous event established on so full of evidence" that it amounts to an entire proof (112). By "entire proof" Hume means a proof based on experience and observation of the kind and amount that would support a high probability of the conclusion that a miracle has occurred. Hume gives several reasons why such evidence has yet to be produced:

13.1 Lack of Trustworthy Witnesses

First, there have been no miracles attested to by a "sufficient number" of trustworthy and celebrated persons, all reporting the same event. Here is Hume's description of such persons: ...

> *[They are] all of such unquestioned good sense, education, and learning, as to secure against all delusion in themselves; of such undoubted integrity as to place them beyond all suspicion of any design to deceive others; of such credit and reputation in the eyes of mankind, as to have a great deal to lose in case of their being detected in any falsehood; and in so celebrated a part of the world, as to render the detection unavoidable (112-113).*

All of these moral attributes are required if we are to accept the testimony of any group of persons about the occurrence of a miracle. Hume declares that such a group is yet to be found "in all history"

(112). In a later paragraph, Hume discusses the testimony of people in "ignorant and barbarous nations." The fact that they are ignorant and barbarous should be a "strong presumption against these stories." Hume here assumes that no group of persons in these nations would meet any of the moral requirements specified in above.

13.2 The Misleading Role of Surprise and Wonder

Second, most events regarded as miracles are the product of surprise and wonder, "giving a sensible tendency toward the belief of these events." Surprise and wonder are agreeable emotions, and most persons will welcome the fantastical stories they are told by others. They also enjoy being among those who pass on such stories to others. But being delighted about something that has happened ("I won the lottery") is not sufficient to declare the event as a miracle. Winning the lottery is highly improbable, but it is also the causal result of natural forces.

13.3 The Contradictions of Religion

Third, the miracles cited by the proponents of different religions contradict one another. The evidence of the miracles testified by Muslims and Christians, for example, "whether weak or strong, are opposite to each other." In matters of religion, "whatever is different is contrary; and ...it is impossible" for all religions, be established on any solid foundation." Hume writes that this argument is the same as that of a judge who refuses to credit the testimony of two witnesses to a criminal act because it is contrary to the testimony of two other witnesses who say that the accused was two hundred miles away "at the same instant when the crime is said to have been committed" (117).

In his *Letters*, Hume writes

> *If a miracle proves a doctrine to be revealed from God, and consequently true, a miracle can never be wrought for a con-*

trary doctrine. The facts are therefore as incompatible as the doctrines. (Greig, Letters I, 350; Gaskin, 117).

Paraphrasing Gaskin (117-118), the form of Hume's argument appears to be this:

1. A set of miracles M1 is claimed to establish the truth of religion R1.

2. A second set of miracles M2 is claimed to establish the truth of religion R2.

3. R1 and R2 are contraries, that is, they cannot both be true (although both could be false).

4. Hence, M1 and M2 cannot both have occurred.

5. Hence, whatever evidence substantiates M1 is contrary to the evidence which substantiates M2, and vice versa.

Professor Gaskin observes that the conclusion of this argument is especially applicable to the differences between monotheistic religions (Judaism, Christianity, Islam) and polytheistic religions (the religions of Olympus and Valhalla):

At least for the Christian, evidence of the activity of his God is evidence of the non-existence of the gods of Olympus. These gods cannot exist if the Christian God exists and miracles which might appear to confirm their activity cannot have taken place if the Christian miracles took place (Gaskin, 118-119).

But the conclusion of Hume's argument is also applicable to contrary monotheistic religions. Thus, if both Christianity and Islam contend that there is one and only one God and this god is the god of their religion, then evidence of the activity of the god of Islam (as shown by miracles) is evidence of the non-existence of the god of Christianity, and vice versa.

13.4 No Human Testimony can Prove a Miracle

Hume brings the chapter on miracles to a close with the following powerful conclusion:

> *Upon the whole, then, no testimony for any kind of miracle has ever mounted to a probability much less to a proof; and that, even supposing it amounted to a proof, it would be opposed by another proof; derived from the very nature of the fact, which it would endeavor to establish. It is experience only, which gives authority to human testimony; and it is the same experience, which assures us of the laws of nature. When, therefore, these two kinds of experience are contrary, we have nothing to do but subtract the one from the other, with that assurance which arises from the remainder. But according to the principle here explained this subtraction, with regard to all popular religions, amounts to an entire annihilation; and therefore we may establish it as a maxim, that no human testimony can have such force as to prove a miracle, and make it a just foundation for any such system of religion (122).*

Hume gives the example of two historical records. (1) The first recounts the testimony of "all authors, in all languages" who agree that, "from the first of January 1600, there was a total darkness over the whole earth for eight days." Hume writes that "instead of doubting the fact, [we] ought to receive it as certain, and ought to search for the causes whence it might be derived."

Now compare this with (2) a second report, also agreed to by all historians, that on the first of January 1600, Queen Elizabeth died. Her death was witnessed by her physicians and the whole court. But after being interred a month, "she again appeared, resumed the throne, and governed England for three years."

Hume responds to (2) with the remark that "I should not have the least inclination to believe so miraculous an event." Although he would not doubt of the queen's "pretended death," and the public circumstances that followed it, "I should only assert it to have been pretended, and that it neither was, nor possibly could be real." He admits that he would be surprised and astonished that anyone would attempt to "deceive the world in an affair of such consequence," but "would still reply, that the knavery and folly of men are of such common phenomena, that I should rather believe the most extraordinary events to arise from their concurrence, than admit of so signal a violation of the laws of nature" (123).

Hume's point is that the amount of testimony in support of the claim that a miracle has occurred would have to be "incredibly large before it can possibly offset the weight of the evidence against the event drawn from our past experience" (Rowe, 140). This sets a very high bar. The falsehood of the testimony must be more miraculous than the event to which it testifies. If historians tell us that physicians and the court were witness to the death and resurrection of Queen Elizabeth in 1600, then "we are obliged to compare the instances of the violation of truth in the testimony of people, with those of the violations of the law of nature by miracles, in order to judge which of them is most likely and probable." (124) We know from experience that it is far more likely that the queen did not die and later rise from the grave than it is likely that the witnesses are telling the truth. To repeat: the evidence from experience against the occurrence of a miracle is extremely strong. Hence, the evidence for a miracle is always extremely weak. Second, if there is a miracle, then there is not only a transgression of the law of nature but the transgression occurred only because there has been an intervention of God or some other invisible agent. But how is this to be verified or falsified? What is the test for determining that it is either true or false that an "invisible agent" intervened? If there is no answer to this question, then we would not be remiss in rejecting any claim about divine intervention, and subsequently any claim that a miraculous event has occurred.

Questions for thought and discussion

1. How does Hume define the word "miracle"? What are some of the objections to his definition?

2. Why does Hume argue that it is never reasonable to believe that a miracle has occurred?

3. Suppose one can prove that a violation of a law of nature has occurred. Is this sufficient to prove that the violation is a miracle?

4. Scientists often reject and revise laws in the light of exceptions, and they do not regard these exceptions as miracles. Has Hume overestimated the weight that should be given to past experience in support of some principle thought to be a law of nature? Is there a way to make revisions of a law of nature without referring to these exceptions as "unreasonable"? (Rowe, 143)

5. Hume focused on the question of whether witness testimony should have much weight in deciding whether or not a miracle has occurred. Would he have arrived at the same skeptical result if he had *personally* been witness to an extraordinary event (for example, the resurrection of Thomas Hobbes or John Locke)?

References

BBC News. 19 February 2019. "National Emergency: Is there a Crisis at the U.S.-Mexico Border?" https://www.bbc.com/news/world-us-canada-44319094

Dorland's Illustrated Medical Dictionary, 31st Edition. 2007. www.Dorland.com

Flew, Antony. 1961. Hume's Philosophy of Belief, Chapter VIII. London: Routledge & Kegan Paul.

Gaskin, J.C.A. 1978. Hume's Philosophy of Religion. New York: Macmillan.

Greig, J.Y.T. (ed.). 1932. The Letters of David Hume. Oxford: Oxford University Press.

Robbins, Rebecca. 20 February 2017. "FDA Issues Warning About Young Blood Transfusions". Scientific American. https://www.scientificamerican.com/article/fda-issues-warning-about-young-blood-transfusions/

Shostak, Seth. 20 February 2019. "Unidentified flying object" https://www.britannica.com/topic/unidentified-flying-object

University of University of Nebraska. 2019. Astronomy Education: Kepler Laws. https://astro.unl.edu/naap/pos/pos_background1.html

IV A GUIDE TO *OF THE IMMORTALITY OF THE SOUL*

CHAPTER FOURTEEN

14. IMMORTALITY: A BELIEF THAT NEVER DIES

[The full text of Hume's *Of the Immortality of the Soul* is reprinted in Appendix B]

The belief in immortality and life after death is as old as religion itself. It is found in Christianity, Islam, in some versions of Judaism and in many other religious belief systems. It is also found in ancient philosophy. Democritus, Epictetus, Socrates and Plato not only believed in the existence of a life after death, but they gave reasoned arguments for this belief. In the early modern era of philosophy (1500--1800 AD), the rationalist philosophers Descartes, Leibniz and Spinoza, joined by the empiricist John Locke all endorsed and argued for a life after death. David Hume was one of the rare scholars of this era to question the idea.

In a 2014 CBS News poll, the most recent on the subject, sixty-six percent of respondents said they believed in heaven and hell, ten percent believed in heaven only, and about seventeen percent said they believed in neither. The belief in an afterlife is not always tied to religion, although the numbers who harbor such beliefs are smaller for atheists and agnostics. In a 2013 Pew poll, twenty-seven percent of agnostics and thirteen percent of atheists said they believed in some kind of afterlife. As for what kind of afterlife, almost fifty percent of non-religious people polled say they believe in neither heaven nor hell, while thirty six percent believe in both and seven percent of non-religious persons believe in heaven only. "Americans who don't identify with any particular religion or are atheist or agnostic are much less likely to say they believe in either heaven or hell" (Weldon, 2014).

The fact that a-majority of Americans believe in life after death might explain the recent rise in the number of books that have been published on the topic. Where there were only a few books in the 20th century promoting the probable existence of an afterlife, there are now over 200 books about an afterlife on sale, most assuring their readers that they can look forward to living a second life after they die.

The major difference between most of the new books and almost all of the older tomes on immortality and life after death is that the many of the new books purport to base their conclusions on *evidence*, not on religious authority. Several of them even use the word "science" in the title or subtitle. The evidence they cite is taken from near-death experiences or other kinds of experiences that the authors and/or others have had in this life, from which they draw the conclusion that it is either certain or at least highly probable that there is a new life awaiting us after we die.

Almost none of recent popular books is skeptical about the existence of an afterlife. But what I found most astonishing while examining the arguments presented by the leading pro-after-life authors, it would appear that none have ever read David Hume's famous contribution to the debate. And this is my reason for writing a postscript to this chapter, using Hume's principles as a guide.

14.1 What Does it Mean to Believe in Life After Death?

In his book *Immortality*, the philosopher Paul Edwards described several different questions answered by those who believe in an afterlife.

The first difference Edwards found is between those who want to know whether human beings survive the death of their bodies or whether humans are (somehow) immortal. Answers to the first question do not also answer the latter. A belief in survival after death could be paired with a belief in eventual total annihilation. A belief in immortality on the other hand, "makes the stronger claim that human beings will go on living forever" (Edwards, 2). And if one accepts Plato's idea that the soul of a person existed eternally before physical birth, then immortality makes the even stronger claim that human beings have previously lived forever.

Second, there are those who ask whether the individual will survive intact, or whether after death, humans will lose their individuality and merge with some kind of Absolute or Cosmic Mind.

Third, there are questions about the vehicle of survival after death. Does one survive as a disembodied mind (a soul), will one survive death with a body, perhaps the body she had prior to death or in a different body? Or is there a third way of surviving death that does not necessarily involve either a disembodied mind or a physical body?

Fourth, where does one go after death? What is the place of survival? Heaven, hell or reincarnation in a new body?

Fifth, who survives death? Only humans? Or do dogs, cats, rodents and other animals also survive death? And if only humans survive death, do all or only some humans survive?

14.2 Three Arguments for Immortality

With reference to Edwards' distinctions, David Hume restricts his answers to questions about the immortality of a disembodied soul. Hume also comments on the "justice" of punishments in the afterlife, the possibility of non-human immortality, and the difficulty of finding places where immortal souls might reside.

Like any cautious philosopher, Hume lays out different approaches that believers have used when attempting to prove that the human soul is immortal. He divides these approaches into three categories: metaphysical, physical and moral. Of these categories, he regards as philosophical only the physical arguments for immortality.

14.2.1 Metaphysical Arguments

> *"Metaphysical topics are founded on the supposition that the soul is immaterial, and that it is impossible for thought to belong to a material substance"*

The question that Hume raises in this section is whether the supposition is coherent. Does it make any sense to say that the soul is immortal because it is classified as an immaterial substance?

Some metaphysicians have argued that the soul is a substance that has no physical properties, for example, color, weight, height, shape. Only material objects (chairs, houses. rocks, and trees) are substances possessing physical properties: large or small, tall or short, rectangular or square, blue or green. The body of a human being is also a substance, distinguished by physical properties, for example, height, shape and color. But the soul, as metaphysicians like Descartes and Locke conceive it, is non-physical. It has no shape, weight or color. Although the soul is a substance, it has only mental properties, for example, thoughts, dreams, imaginings, and the feelings of pleasure and pain.

Dualism is the name of the philosophical theory that holds that a person is composed of two different substances: mind and body. The human body is the material substance in which the non-material soul (mind) resides when the body is alive. Material substance can change, be destroyed or die. A person's body is a material substance that will suffer radical changes over time as the body ages. At some time during this process the body will die. But the substance called "soul" or "mind" that allegedly resides within the living body does not die. As a non-physical substance *by definition* it cannot change or suffer destruction or death. When the body dies, the mind may cease to have thoughts and feelings, but *qua* substance, the soul cannot be destroyed, precisely because it is non-physical (immaterial).

Now according to the argument in the quotation above, thought has to belong somewhere. It is impossible for a thought to belong to the body because the body is a material substance and thoughts are immaterial. The thoughts that you are now having as you read these words cannot be observed by others. You can think about the color red but your thought is not red. You can think about height and weight, but your thought is not tall or short, heavy or light. If a team of physicians opens your skull, they can see your material brain but they cannot see your thoughts. They can measure the electrical and chemical composition of the gray matter, but they cannot observe and measure the thoughts that somehow exist "in" the gray matter. It follows from these considerations that thoughts must belong to an immaterial substance, and that substance is called the soul.

But just metaphysics teaches us, that the notion of substance is wholly confused and imperfect, and that we have no other idea of any substance, than as an aggregate of particular qualities inhering in an unknown something. Matter, therefore, and spirit, are at bottom equally unknown, and we cannot determine what qualities may inhere in the one or the other.

The philosopher who Hume must have in mind is his predecessor John Locke, who said this about substance:

The idea that we have, to which we give the general name substance, being nothing, but the supposed, but unknown support of those qualities, we find existing, which we imagine cannot subsist, sine re substante, without something to support them, we call that support substantia, which, according to the true import of the word, is in plain English, standing under or upholding. (II xxiii 2)

Substance, then, is an unknown support of mental and physical properties. Locke continue with this passage:

We have as clear a notion of the substance of spirit as we have of body: the one being supposed to be (without knowing what it is) the substratum to those simple ideas we have from without;

> *and the other supposed (with a like ignorance of what it is) to be the substratum to those operations which we experiment in ourselves within. 'Tis plain then, that the idea of corporeal substance in matter, is as remote from our conceptions, and apprehensions, as that of spiritual substance, or spirit;... (II 23 v)*

Returning to the opening quote from Hume, if we have no knowledge about the notion of substance, then we have no reason to think that thought and other mental properties inhere in material or in immaterial substance, that is, in body or mind. It follows from this that we cannot know whether matter, "by its structure and arrangement, may not be the cause of thought." We cannot know a priori whether one thing is the cause of another. Hence, we cannot know a priori whether matter or spirit is the cause of thought. Only experience can settle questions about cause and effect. But if the notion of the substance of spirit and of body is unknown, then we cannot know whether either one or these or both is the cause of thinking, remembering, imagining, etc.

If it is insisted that the idea of spiritual substance or the idea of soul is meaningful, then (Hume asserts), "nature uses it after the manner she does the other substance, matter":

> *As the same material substance may successively compose the bodies of all animals, the same spiritual substance may compose their minds: Their consciousness, or that system of thought which they formed during life, may be continually dissolved by death; and nothing interest them in the new modification. ... And that an immaterial substance, as well as a material, may lose its memory or consciousness, appears, in part, from experience, if the soul be immaterial.*

Think about it this way: if you and I and everyone else have the same material substance in which our physical properties inhere (height, weight, color, etc.), then by analogy, we all have the same spiritual substance which serves as the support of our mental properties (thoughts, dreams, imaginings, etc.). It also follows by analogy that as a material substance may lose its physical properties over time, so may the spiritual substance (soul) lose its mental properties. And there is some empirical evidence that this what happens, as when a person suffers from dementia, retrograde amnesia or Alzheimer's disease.

Hume concludes his discussion of metaphysical topics with the remark that "whatever is incorruptible is also ingenerable" (i.e. if something cannot be destroyed, then it cannot be generated). This implies that a soul, "if immortal, existed before our birth." There is no time at which our soul did not exist and there is no time at which it will cease to exist. "And if the former existence nowise concerned us, neither will the latter."

And why, Hume asks, do we restrict those who possess immaterial and immortal souls to the human species? Surely animals "feel, think, love, hate, will, and even reason, though in a more imperfect manner than a man." These mental properties require a substratum in which they inhere. There is no reason for thinking that the human substratum is any different than the substratum supporting animal properties. Hence, when your dog or cat dies, their soul, which existed before they were born, will continue to exist.

14.2.2 Moral Arguments

Hume now turns to consider the moral arguments, chiefly those arguments derived from the justice of God, who is alleged to be interested in the further punishment of the vicious and the reward of the virtuous in the afterlife.

Hume's reference is to the God of Christianity, a being who is declared by believers to possess all perfections, including the perfection of being all-good. On a standard of virtue, God would be at the top. Indeed, it is God who created the standard and enforces it by divine commands backed by threats of punishment and rewards in the afterlife to those who meet or fail to meet the minimum standard of virtue.

The moral argument for immortality goes something like this:

1. If God is all-good then God would create human beings who have immortal souls.

2. God (by definition) is all-good.

3. Therefore, God has created human beings who have immortal souls.

The proof of the first premise is that given a choice between being mortal and being immortal, it is better that God gave humans immortality. Or more precisely, it is better that humans are endowed with immortal souls. It is better to have a soul that goes on living forever than to have a soul that suffers complete annihilation. Why?

Christians have an answer to this question. They would first say that an act is morally wrong only if it violates a commandment of God. Second, morally wrong acts are eternally punished in the afterlife and morally right acts are eternally rewarded. Therefore, a belief in immortality gives one a much stronger motive for doing what God commands in this life than the motive that one would have if one believed that one's soul is mortal. Hence, persons who are about to violate God's command are more likely to refrain from immoral behavior. They will refrain because they believe that their immoral act will be punished in the afterlife (hell). They will do what God commands because they also believe that the life of a righteous person will be rewarded in the afterlife (heaven).

This is where Hume enters the debate. He has six objections.

14.2.2.1 The Injustice of Double Jeopardy

The first objection starts with Hume's point that violators of God's law are not only punished in this life; they are also punished in the afterlife. The latter punishment is threatened to be much more severe.

Here is Hume's passionate response to this duality of punishment:

> *What cruelty, what iniquity, what injustice in nature, to confine thus all our concern, as well as all our knowledge, to the present life, if there be another scene still awaiting us, of infinitely greater consequence? Ought this barbarous deceit to be ascribed to a beneficent and wise being?*

A beneficent God would not add an additional punishment in the afterlife to the punishment previously meted out to for violators of the law in the present life, especially if God's punishment is "of infinitely greater consequence." It is "a barbarous deceit" to give multiple punishments for the same crime.

14.2.2.2 The Injustice of a Failure to Promulgate

Second, if God is just, then God's commands would be transparent and promulgated to all. However, we have no idea in this life "by what rule punishments and rewards [are] distributed" in the afterlife nor do we know with any certainty the "Divine Standard of merit and demerit." There is a great deal of dispute about such matters between Catholics and Protestants and certainly between Christians and a multitude of believers from other religions.

John Locke makes a different point about the pre-political law of nature (the Divine standard) in *Second Treatise of Government*. He contends that the natural law is "plain and intelligible to all rational creatures." Locke puts the blame on human beings who either remain ignorant of the natural law ("for want of study of it"), or who want only to promote their own private interests, despite what they believe the natural law tells them to do or not to do.

14.2.2.3 Divine Punishment has no Purpose

Third, Hume surmises that there appears to be no moral purpose to divine punishment.

> *Punishment, without any proper end or purpose, is inconsistent with our ideas of goodness and justice; and no end can be served by it after the whole scene is closed.*

Punishment should have an end or purpose, whether it be deterrence or therapy. But what could be the purpose of punishing someone in the afterlife if those in the present life have no access to what is happening to the souls of the deceased? Surely the purpose of divine punishment of a thief in the afterlife could not deter anyone from committing the same crime in this life, especially if everything they know about the afterlife has been "artificially fostered by precept and education."

14.2.2.4 Divine Punishment is not Proportional to the Offense

Punishment, according to our conceptions, should bear some proportion to the offense.

> *Why then eternal punishment for the temporary offenses of so frail a creature as man?*

According to the retributive theory of punishment, justice demands that the severity of a punishment should be proportionate to the seriousness of the crime. Why then would the crime for which a person has already been punished in this life deserve eternal torture in the afterlife? Eternal punishment is an extreme violation of what everyone regards as "just" punishment.

14.2.2.5 Divine Examination of Children for Possible Sins

Fifth, it is absurd to assume that children are possible sinners who must be placed in a probationary state after death.

> *Nature has rendered human infancy peculiarly frail and mortal; as it were on purpose to refute the notion of a probationary state. The half of mankind die before they are rational creatures.*

Children lack the capacity to understand the moral law and conform to its rules. They are not "rational creatures." A beneficent God would not create humans who are "frail and mortal" or who suffer early death only to subject them to a probationary state in which they are examined for any alleged sins.

14.2.2.6 Determinism and Human Responsibility

> *As every effect implies a cause, and that another, till we reach the first cause of all, which is the Deity; everything that happens, is ordained by him; and nothing can be the object of his punishment or vengeance.*

Hume's sixth and final moral objection to the Christian idea of divine punishment starts with the observation that whether for the purpose of deterrence or retribution, punishment is justified only if the person being punished had the capacity to refrain from the criminal act. But if God is the first or ultimate cause of every act of those who violate the law, then they are not responsible for what they have done. Hence, a just God would not punish nor seek vengeance upon them.

The conclusion that Hume draws from 14.2.2.1 to 14.2.2.6 is that the Christian view of immortality "of the type popularly and traditionally supposed is flagrantly contrary to all human moral decencies" (Gaskin, 101).

14.2.3 Physical arguments for Immortality

Supposing that the theory of immortality of the soul is meaningful, Hume here gives two reasons why he believes it to be false.

> *The physical arguments from the analogy of nature are strong for the mortality of the soul: and those are really the only philosophical arguments, which ought to be admitted with regard to this question, or indeed any question of fact.*

Hume reminds the reader that any question about a matter of fact cannot be answered by an analysis of concepts. For example, I cannot know when the train will arrive at the station by contemplating the concept of "train." I can only know this by consulting the time table and asking the clerk at the station whether the train will arrive on time today. The clerk's answer will depend on his present and past experience of the train's progress. In arriving at the answer, the clerk will depend on an analogy between past and future events; in this case, the assumed analogy is between the speed of the train, the condition of the tracks, times of passenger boarding and several other variables occurring today and similar events that have occurred in the past.

14.2.3.1 Proportional changes of body and mind

Hume argues that the question of the mortality or immortality of the soul is a question of fact. As such, we will not find our answer by examining the concept of "soul." Instead, we must look for an "analogy of nature." Hume suggests the following rule:

> *Where any two objects are so closely connected, that all alterations, which we have ever seen in the one, are attended with proportionable alterations in the other: we ought to conclude, by all rules of analogy, that, when there are still greater alterations produced in the former, and it is totally dissolved, there follows a total dissolution of the latter.*

The best examples are from medical discoveries about cause and effect. There are medications that shrink brain tumors, and in some cases, will dissolve the tumors entirely. Trials for testing medications will be interpreted following rules of analogy. If researchers discover from carefully constructed trials that all alterations in the amount of a medication are proportional to the size of the tumor, then they would be justified in concluding that when they increase the amount, the tumor will disappear over time.

It might be objected that the medical example is about a causal connection between parts of the body whereas Hume's query is about the causal connection between body and mind. But Hume would insist that this is not relevant.

> *The weakness of the body and that of the mind in infancy are exactly proportioned; their vigor in manhood, their sympathetic disorder in sickness, their common gradual decay in old age. The step further seems unavoidable; their common dissolution in death ... What reason then to imagine, that an immense alteration, such as is made on the soul by the dissolution of the body, and all its organs of thought and sensation, can be affected without the dissolution of the whole?*

The analogy between proportional alterations in body and mind in the past allow us to infer that greater alterations in the body will lead to greater alterations in the mind until both are "totally dissolved," that is, they both cease to exist.

14.2.3.2 The Souls of Animals

> *The souls of animals are allowed to be mortal: and these bear so near a resemblance to the souls of men, that the analogy from one to the other forms a very strong argument.*

If we are prepared to say that the bodies of men and the bodies of animals are mortal because the anatomy of a human being bears a strong resemblance to the anatomy of an animal, then we should also be prepared to say that the souls of human beings are mortal because the soul of a human being bears a strong resemblance to the souls of animals: "Animals undoubtedly feel, think, love, hate, will, and even reason, though in a more imperfect manner than man."

14.2.3.3 The Changing Nature of the Soul

Hume writes:

> *Nothing in this world is perpetual. Everything, however seemingly firm, is in continual flux and change: The world itself gives symptoms of frailty and dissolution: How contrary to analogy, therefore, to imagine, that one single form, seeming the frailest of any, and from the objects and causes subject to the greatest disorders, is immortal and indissoluble? What a daring theory is that! How lightly, not to say how rashly, entertained!*

The word "form" in the quote means "soul." Hume's point is that there is as much change in the soul as there is in the body: He earlier used the words "disorder, weakness, insensibility and stupidity" to describe changes in the mind. Today, when describing the psychological symptoms of dementia, we would use the words anxiety, loneliness, mood swings, nervousness, depression, hallucination, and paranoia.

14.2.3.4 The Problem of Soul Disposal

Hume asks: "How to dispose of the infinite number of posthumous existences?" He argues that this is a question that "ought also to embarrass the religious theory." Assuming that "every planet, in every solar system, ...is peopled with intelligent mortal beings," then either a new universe must be created every generation for the disposal of the souls of these beings, or a "prodigiously wide" universe has been previously created to accommodate "this continual influx of beings."

Hume brought up an identical argument in his famous death-bed interview with James Boswell. Boswell writes: "This appeared to me an unphilosophical objection, and I said, 'Mr. Hume, you know spirit does not take up space'" (Schwartz).

14.3 Postscript: A Humean Response to Recent Scientific Proofs of an Afterlife

The twenty-first century has seen a surge in the number of books that attempt to scientifically prove the existence of an afterlife. These books use the word "scientific" to mean that there is empirical evidence for the existence of an afterlife in the near-death experiences reported by persons who are dying or who have been declared clinically dead and later revived. The most common near-death experiences (NDEs) mentioned are out of body experiences in which a near death person has visual and auditory perceptions of their physical body lying on an operating table, as if they are "floating" above it while nurses and physicians are working to revive her. Another type of reported experience is a visual perception of bright lights that appear to emanate from a tunnel that they enter or are about to enter, accompanied by feelings of peace, happiness and even joy.

Near death experiences are put forward as evidence for the conclusion that there is an afterlife because (it is claimed) the NDE is an experience of an afterlife event (e.g. seeing bright lights and tunnels, seeing one's own body on the operating table). It is the soul of a deceased person who is now in the afterlife viewing her own body on the operating table. And it is the bright lights and tunnel emanating from the afterlife that are the cause of the near-death visual experiences of these phenomena.

The immediate objection to this line of reasoning is that an NDE is best explained by the theory that it is a brain event, that is, it is a hallucination caused by electrical and chemical changes occurring in the brain. But this response is immediately countered with the claim that it is biologically impossible (highly improbable) for the brain to function after death. Here is the argument:

1. An NDE is caused either by a brain event or by a non-physical event occurring in an afterlife.

2. It is clinically impossible (i.e. highly improbable) for an NDE to be caused by a brain event.

Therefore,

3. An NDE is caused by a non-physical event occurring in an afterlife

Let us assume that there is a large number of people who have reported identical or nearly identical NDEs of the type reported above: out of body experiences and experiences of bright lights and tunnels. The first question we should ask is whether it is possible that an NDE is an effect (evidence) of a cause occurring in the afterlife. Is this a viable alternative, as stated in premise (1)? Hume puts the question this way in the penultimate paragraph of his essay on immortality:

> *By what arguments or analogies can we prove any state of existence, which no one ever saw, and which no wise resembles any that ever was seen?*

The answer to Hume's question is that the afterlife is "out of the common experienced course of nature." We cannot prove any state of existence that no one ever saw. No one has ever seen any events occurring in an afterlife. And if someone responds that those who are near death are seeing such events, then this begs the question "Is there an afterlife?" Hence, there is no way to prove that afterlife events are the cause of near-death experiences. We cannot prove this "by arguments and analogies" because no one has ever experienced or observed a state of existence that will serve as the analogy. We know what observations we can make and what experiments we can perform to prove that NDEs are the product of electrical and chemical changes in the brain. We have no idea of what experiments we can perform to prove that NDEs are caused by events going on in the afterlife.

As Hume points out again and again, an argument to prove that one event is the cause of another must be analogical and therefore must be based on past experience (2.7.3 *supra*) For example, if my doctor tells me that my migraines are probably caused by stress, then he should be able to show me experimental data that people who are known to be under stress are more likely get migraine headaches than people who are not under stress. But compare this reasoning with that of a psychic who tells me that my migraines are probably caused by my deceased Uncle Oscar. If I ask the psychic to show me the data proving that migraines are likely to be caused by a deceased person, she would not be able to comply with my request. As Hume would put it, no one has ever observed a state of existence in which a deceased being is the cause of a living human being's headache.

The same can be said for the suggestion that near-death experiences are caused by events occurring in an afterlife. There are no experiments that can be performed and no observations that can be made to prove this kind of cause and effect relationship. As Hume so elegantly puts it:

> *Who will repose such trust in any pretended philosophy as to admit upon its testimony the reality of so marvelous a scene? Some new species of logic is requisite for that purpose; and some new faculties of the mind, that they may enable us to comprehend that logic.*

Until we find this new species of logic, I would recommend that we take David Hume's advice and declare as incomprehensible any suggestion that near-death experiences are experiences of events occurring in an afterlife .

Questions for thought and discussion

1. In his discussion of metaphysical arguments for immortality, Hume writes that in the same way that a material substance may lose its physical properties over time, so may the spiritual substance (soul) lose its mental properties. What conclusion follows from this analogy? How would you challenge the analogy?

2. If the question of the mortality or immortality of the soul is a question of fact, then what facts are relevant to finding an answer this question?

3. The seventeenth century philosopher Rene Descartes believed that the "lower" animals did not have souls. When an injured dog cried out in pain, Descartes surmised that unlike humans, the dog does not feel pain any more than a clock feels pain when it makes mechanical noises caused by rusty parts. Is Descartes right about this? How would Hume respond?

4. Is it logically possible that there is a place where souls go after death? Is it also logically possible that someday this place might become too crowded (as suggested by Hume)?

5. Hume argues that an all-good God would not create an immortal human soul. Do you agree

References

Edwards, Paul. 1997. Immortality. New York: Prometheus Books.

Long, Jeffrey, M.D. 2010. Evidence of the Afterlife: The Science of Near-Death Experiences.

Locke, John. Second Treatise of Government.

Payne, Linda. 2019. Health in England (16th – 18th century). Children and Youth in History. http://chnm.gmu.edu/cyh/primary-sources/166

Schwartz, Richard B. 1991. Boswell and Hume: the deathbed interview. Cambridge University Press. https://www.cambridge.org/core/books/new-light-on-boswell/boswell-and-hume-the-deathbed-interview/0D8E152BD8E6B10EB738C899E07D5238

Weldon, Kathleen. 2014. Huffington Post. https://www.huffingtonpost.com/kathleen-weldon/paradise-polled-americans_b_7587538.html

V A GUIDE TO *OF SUICIDE*

CHAPTER FIFTEEN

15. IS SUICIDE IMMORAL?

[The full text of Hume's *Of Suicide* is reprinted in Appendix C]

Reports of suicide often make their way into the newspapers, television and radio news programs, and are discussed and widely disseminated on social media. A daily recitation of these events is a litany of human tragedy. A famous author takes her life because she has been diagnosed with Alzheimer's Disease. She cannot bear the gradual deterioration of the skills that led to her best-selling novels, nor does she want to be a burden to her husband. A teenager hangs herself after being constantly bullied at school and on social media. An elderly man kills himself after the recent death of his wife of 60 years, explaining in a note "I do not want to live without her." A movie star takes his life because he cannot bear the constant terrible bouts of depression.

After two paragraphs in which Hume praises philosophy for freeing persons from "superstition and false religion," he informs his readers that he will "restore their native liberty by examining all the common arguments against Suicide." In doing this he disputes Christian doctrine and sides with the ancient philosophers, most of whom declared that it is never immoral for a person to commit suicide.

Christian doctrine is based on the writings of St. Augustine and St. Thomas Aquinas who offered the first justifications of the prohibition on suicide (Cholbi, citing Amundson). The ancient philosophers cited by Hume are Seneca, Tacitus and Pliny, each of them arguing that suicide is morally justifiable. In the modern era, the philosopher John Locke took the Christian position and

argued that because human beings are created by God, they are his property, "... made to last during his, not one another's pleasure" (*Second Treatise*, §6). It follows that killing oneself is wrong for the same reason that committing arson is wrong: it is a property crime committed against God. In the eighteenth century, Immanuel Kant agreed with Locke that suicide is morally wrong but for a different reason. He argued that a moral law permitting suicide would endorse a contradictory system of nature that "would destroy life by means of the very same feeling that acts so as to stimulate life" (*Grounding*, 422).

In his posthumous essay "Of Suicide" (reprinted in Appendix C), David Hume does not question the motives of those who have committed suicide, nor does he give advice to those who are contemplating this final act. Instead, he critically examines arguments for the conclusion that suicide is always *morally* wrong.

Hume organizes the essay on suicide by considering and answering three questions: Is suicide (1) a violation of one's duty to God? (2) a violation of a duty not to cause harm to others, or (3) a violation of a duty to oneself?

15.1 Suicide and Duties to God

Hume begins with the remark that there are "general and immutable laws" established by God which govern everything that happens in the material world, from the movement of a leaf in the wind to the motion of a planet. God also governs the animal world (all living creatures) by giving them bodily and mental powers (senses, passions, appetites, memory and judgement) by which "they are impelled and regulated in the course of life to which they are destined." The material and animal worlds sometimes come into conflict – they "mutually retard or forward each other's operations." A rushing river might prevent a person from crossing her path, and the same river might be manipulated by man in such a way that it powers generators of electricity.

All events, in one sense, "may be pronounced [as] the action of the almighty; they all proceed from those powers [material and animal] with which he has endowed his creatures." It will do no good to protest that when a house is deliberately destroyed by the hands of man this is different than when a house is destroyed by falling of its own weight. A man, it might be said, tears down the house because this is what he wants to do according to his own plan, and he directs his body to carry out this task. Surely this process differs significantly from a house that simply collapses according to the laws of motion and gravitation. To this Hume replies:

> *When the passions play, when the judgment dictates, when the limbs obey; this is all the operation of God, and upon these animate principles, as well as upon the inanimate, [God] has established the government of the universe... There is no event, however important to us, which [God] has exempted from the general laws that govern the universe, or which he has peculiarly received for his own immediate action and operation.*

It is important to understand that when Hume uses the phrase "general laws that govern the universe," he does not mean prescriptive laws as in, for example, the Ten Commandments, the provisions of the U.S. Constitution, the statutes and laws of states and cities that govern the behavior of citizens, and other laws that command our obedience under pain of punishment. Nor is he referring to Locke's natural law condemning suicide. The "general laws" that Hume is discussing are the laws of science. They are descriptive: they describe the regular behavior of material objects in the universe, for example, the motion of the planets orbiting around the sun. (The planet Venus keeps to its orbit not because it fears that it will be punished if it should stray, but because it is subject to the forces of gravity and inertia, as described in Kepler's Laws of Planetary Motion.) Because of the regularity of their motion through space, the position of the planets at any given time can be accurately predicted.

Animal behavior, including human behavior, is also governed by descriptive general laws. Like the behavior of material matter, the word "governed" does not mean "prescribed." For example, based on past experience and observation of animal behavior, the law of self-preservation says that we can predict the high probability that an animal will take steps to prevent itself from being harmed or killed. The law does not say that an animal *ought* to preserve its own life, has a moral obligation to preserve its own life, or that it is morally wrong not to do this.

One reason why readers might confuse prescriptive and descriptive general laws can be traced to Hume's declaration that everything that happens in the universe is a direct consequence of God's plan and design. There are gravitational forces at work because this is how God has planned the movement of material objects; animals instinctively do what they can to avoid injury or death because this is how God has designed animal behavior.

There is also a historical reason for confusing prescriptive and descriptive general laws. Thomas Hobbes describes the first law of nature as "a precept or general rule, found out by reason, by which a man is forbidden to do that which is destructive of his life, or taketh away the means of preserving the same; and to omit that, by which he thinketh it may be best preserved" (Leviathan, Chapter 14, sect. 3, p. 79). John Locke states that the fundamental law of nature is that as much as possible, mankind is to be preserved, thus implying that everyone has a duty to preserve one's self (Second Treatise, 2.6). In both cases, the law of self-preservation is construed as prescriptive, not descriptive. And with specific reference to suicide, Locke argued that because human beings are created by God, they are his property, "... made

to last during his, not one another's pleasure" (Second Treatise, §6). Hence, suicide is wrong not only because it violates the duty to preserve one's own life but it violates the duty not to annihilate property that belongs to the Creator.

Hume has a different approach to suicide. If there is no event which God has exempted from the general laws that govern the universe, and suicide is an event, then the taking of one's own life is not exempt from the general laws regulating animal behavior. Hume cites the example of "a man who, tired of life, and hunted by pain and misery, bravely overcomes all the natural terrors of death and makes his escape from this cruel scene." Why should we think of this act as a transgression of the general laws? Has this man "incurred the indignation of his creator by encroaching on the office of divine providence, and disturb[ed] the order of the universe?" This question wrongly assumes that the general laws are prescriptive. The correct answer is that there is no more that this person or any person can do that will transgress or violate the general laws governing behavior than a robot programmed to take out the trash on Mondays can do. The man who takes his own life may be doing something that is unusual or extraordinary, but the fact that it happens at all is proof of its consistency with the general laws.

> *The lives of men depend upon the same laws as the lives of all other animals; and these are subjected to the general laws of matter and motion. ...[Therefore,] it is no encroachment on the office of providence to disturb or alter these general laws. Everyone, of consequence [has] the free disposal of his own life [and] ... lawfully employ[s] that power with which nature has endowed him.*

Thus, the man who "makes his escape" from life by committing suicide has done an act that is explainable and potentially predictable by general laws. Suicide is certainly not a miraculous act. Unlike

Hume's definition of a miracle (in *Of Miracles*, reprinted below), a suicide not only does not transgress general laws, it is perfectly consistent with them.

Much empirical evidence suggests that outright self-destructiveness is often found in highly social species like our own in which there is a conjunction of low residual reproductive potential and burdensomeness toward kin (De Cantanzaro, 1991).

Hume observes that if the almighty had declared that taking one's own life is morally wrong, then "it would be equally criminal to act for the preservation of life." Destroying and preserving one's life are two sides of the same coin: both actions "employ our powers of mind and body, to produce some innovation in the course of nature: and in none of them do any more. They are therefore, all of them, equally innocent or equally criminal."

Hume's argument for the claim that suicide is not morally wrong goes something like this:

    1. It is not morally wrong (a violation of duty) to act according to general law.

    2. Acts of suicide accord with general law.

    3 Therefore, acts of suicide are not morally wrong (a violation of duty).

One might accuse Hume of committing the fallacy of ambiguity in this argument. This fallacy occurs when a word or phrase has different meanings in two or more occurrences. (For example: "If all sharp objects are knives and some cheeses are sharp, then some cheeses are knives.")

In Hume's argument the phrase "general law" in premise (a) means a prescriptive law that tells us the conditions under which suicide is morally wrong. But in premise (b) "general law" refers to a descriptive law that tells us the conditions under which persons are likely to commit suicide. This ambiguity renders the argument invalid.

In defense of Hume, it might be argued that insufficient attention has been paid to Hume's claim that the general laws are created by God. Hence, "it would always be wrong to contravene these laws for the sake of our own happiness. But clearly it is not wrong, since God frequently permits us to contravene these laws, for he does not expect us not to respond to disease or other calamities. Therefore, there is not apparent justification, as Hume put it, for God's permitting us to disturb nature in some circumstances but not in others. "Just as God permits us to divert rivers for irrigation, so too ought he permit us to divert blood from our veins" (Cholbi).

15.2 Suicide and Duties to Others

Hume has a short answer to those who claim that suicide is morally wrong because it violates a universal duty we have not to harm others. His reply is that "he [who commits suicide] only ceases to do good; which, if it is an injury, it is of the lowest kind."

Hume observes that when we have an obligation to do good to society it is because we have received certain benefits. Thus, doing good to society is an act of reciprocity. This implies that we must stay alive, at least as long as it takes to pay our debt to society.

Plato considers a version of the reciprocity argument in the dialogue *Crito* when Socrates responds to Crito's claim that Socrates has an obligation to escape from jail and avoid execution (49c). Socrates responds that his obligation is to obey the laws of Athens, including the law that sets the manner of punishment. He argues that the obligation to obey the law is reciprocal with the implied promise that all citizens make when they freely receive benefits conferred upon them by the state (Crito, 50c – 51e)

But suppose, Hume asks, that I withdraw myself altogether from society and receive no benefits at all. Surely then, I would have no obligation to stay alive, unless the obligation to do good is perpetual. Even then, Hume responds, there must be some limits to my obligations. For example, the good that I could do for society might be minimal and the harm I do to myself by remaining alive is great:

> *Why then should I prolong a miserable existence, because of some frivolous advantage which the public may perhaps receive from me?"* If an elderly and very ill person decides to leave all friends and family in an attempt to *"alleviate as much as possible the miseries"* of the remaining days of her life, why may she not *"cut short these miseries at once by an action [suicide] which is no more prejudicial to society?"*

Hume puts forward several scenarios in which he claims that a person who commits suicide either does no harm or does minimal harm to others. First, because of the seriousness of one's illness (for example, terminal cancer), it may no longer be in a person's power to promote the interests of others. Second, the person is a spy acting for the public interest who is caught and threatened with torture by the enemy unless he divulges his secrets. He "knows from his own weakness that the secret will be extorted from him." Would it not be laudable if this person takes his own life before the torture begins? Third, a convicted murderer awaiting execution might commit suicide in order to avoid "the anguish of thinking" about his approaching death: "His voluntary death is equally advantageous to society by ridding it of a pernicious member."

15.3 Suicide and Duties to Oneself

Hume answers the question as soon as it is asked: "That suicide may often be consistent with interest and with our duty to ourselves, no one can question." Our duty to our self is identical with what is in our own self-interest. "Age, sickness, or misfortune may render life a burden, and make it worse even than annihilation." Thus, there may be occasions in which persons reasonably contemplate suicide, even though they will acknowledge a "natural horror" of death. Suicide is something that one is motivated to do only when one is in the grips of "an incurable depravity or gloominess of temper as must poison all enjoyment, and render [one] equally miserable as if [one] had been loaded with the most grievous misfortune."

Questions for thought and discussion

1. Hume appears to be arguing that if suicide is a natural event governed by general laws, then there is no good reason to conclude that suicide is morally wrong. Is he right about this? Is there a way to interpret Hume that would justify his conclusion about suicide? Explain.

2. Hume argues that the person who commits suicide does not cause harm to others. Is he right about this? What would he say about the emotional damage and loss of financial support suffered by the young children of a single parent who commits suicide?

3. What would Hume say about Immanuel Kant's claim that self-preservation is a fundamental moral duty that would be violated by a person who commits suicide, even if this person killed himself to escape the pain and suffering of the end stages of terminal cancer?

4. Hume does not recommend suicide nor does he tell us the conditions under which suicide might be prudent or wise. Is there anything in his essay that would imply an answer to the question "Is it ever prudent or wise for a person to commit suicide?

References

American Foundation for Suicide Prevention. 2019. Suicide Statistics. https://afsp.org/about-suicide/suicide-statistics/

Aquinas, St. Thomas. 1945 [1273 CE]. Summa Theologica, in Basic Writings of Saint Thomas Aquinas, Anton Pegis (ed.), New York: Random House.

Augustine, St., 1958 [c. 413-426 CE]. City of God, Gerald G. Walsh, Demetrius B. Zema, Grace Monahan, Daniel J. Honan (trans.), Garden City, N.Y.: Image Books.

Brown, R. M., Dahlen, E., Mills, C., Rick, J. and Biblarz, A. 1999. "Evaluation of an Evolutionary Model of Self-Preservation and Self-Destruction". Suicide and Life-Threatening Behavior, 29: 58-71. doi:10.1111/j.1943-278X.1999.tb00763.x

Cholbi, Michael, "Suicide", The Stanford Encyclopedia of Philosophy (Fall 2017 Edition), Edward N. Zalta (ed.), https://plato.stanford.edu/archives/fall2017/entries/suicide/ .

De Cantazaro, Denys. 1991. "Evolutionary limits to self-preservation" Ethology and Sociobiology, 12: 13-28. https://doi.org/10.1016/0162-3095(91)90010-N

Kant, Immanuel. 1981 [1785]. Grounding for the Metaphysics of Morals. Ellington, James W. (trans.). Indianapolis: Hackett.

Locke, John. 1980 [1690]. Second Treatise of Government. C.B. Macpherson (ed.), Indianapolis: Hackett

May, Alexis & Klonsky, E David. 2013. "Assessing Motivations for Suicide Attempts: Development and Psychometric Properties of the Inventory of Motivations for Suicide Attempts." Suicide & life-threatening behavior. 43. 10.1111/sltb.12037.

Turtenwald, Kimberly. 2018. The Two Forces that Keep the Planets in Motion Around the Sun" Sciencing. https://sciencing.com/two-planets-motion-around-sun-8675709.html

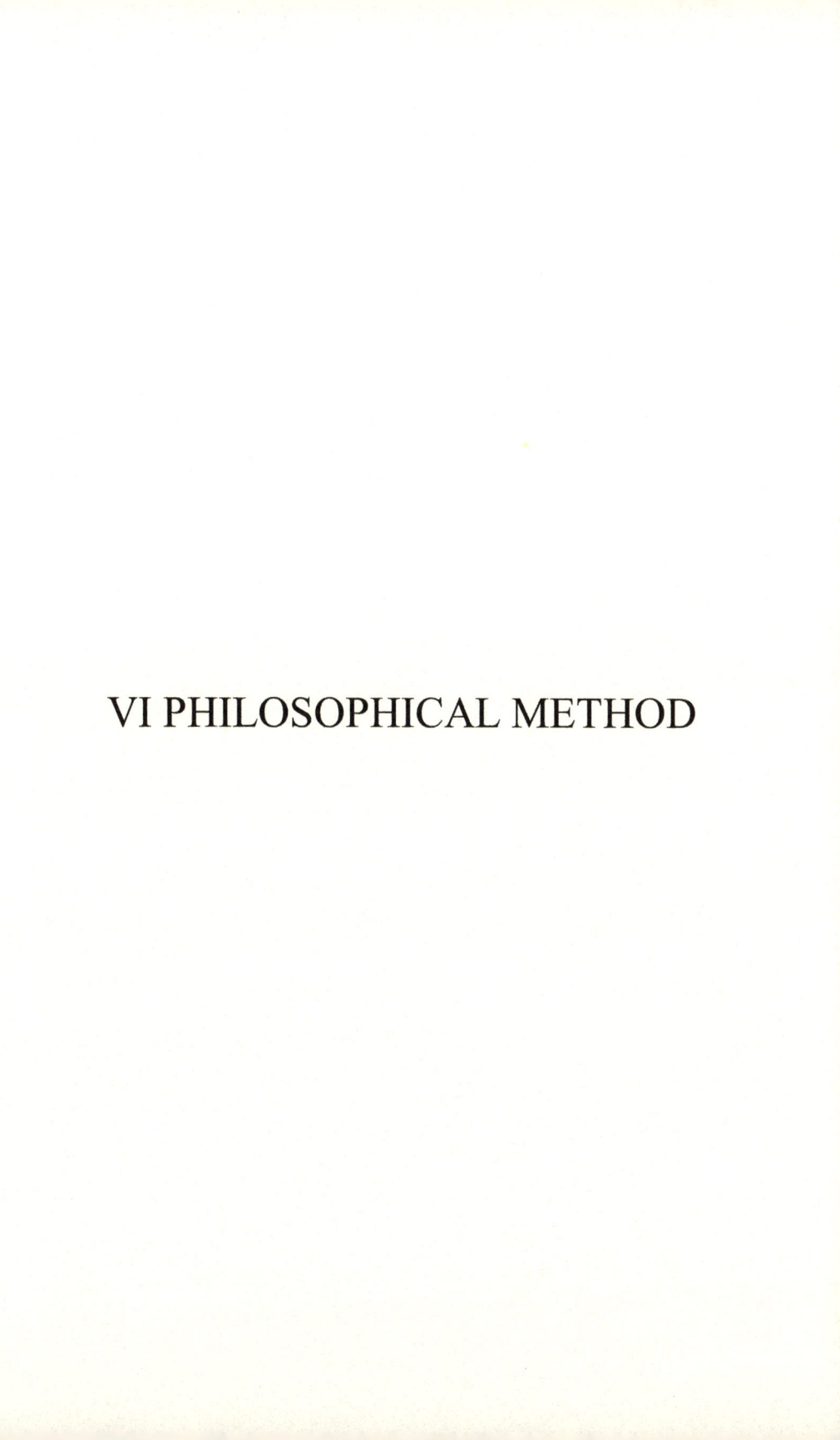

VI PHILOSOPHICAL METHOD

CHAPTER SIXTEEN

16. HUME'S METHODOLOGY

In the previous books in the Smart Student's Guide series we devoted a final chapter showing how the philosopher might answer to the following two questions: "What is philosophy?" and "What is philosophical method?" Philosophers rarely give explicit answers to these questions. David Hume is no exception. Hence, the best we can do is to find answers that are implicit in Hume's critical examination of arguments that have been given on the topics under consideration in this volume: the existence and nature of the Deity, miracles, immortality of the soul, and the common arguments against suicide.

16.1 The Light of Reason

Hume's first sentence in the unpublished essay "Of the Immortality of the Soul" contains the phrase "by the light of reason." Other instances of the word "reason" in his writings are "just reasoning," "sound reason," "rules of good reasoning," "the mere light of reason," "abstract reasoning," "the force of reason," "principles of reasoning" and "method of reasoning."

Hume thinks of reason as a tool to critically examine a controversial argument as in, "By the light of reason it seems difficult to prove the immortality of the soul." It is also used to show the reader how an argument for a conclusion should be supported, as in "sound reason" and "just reasoning." Another use of "reason" is Hume's description of types of reasoning, for example, "abstract reasoning," and his description of the rules and principles of reasoning.

When Hume uses reason as a tool for critical examination, he is applying the rules of logic to the argument at hand. These rules vary depending on whether the argument is a posteriori (inductive) or a priori (deductive). There are several types of arguments a posteriori, but in Dialogues Concerning Natural Religion (DCNR), Hume focuses primarily on analogical arguments in the rigorous examinations therein of the Design Argument for the existence and nature of the deity. Two principles are developed: (a) All inferences concerning fact must be founded on experience; and (b) All experimental reasonings must be founded on the supposition that similar causes prove similar effects. For example, if you infer that the hissing sound you hear is made by the teapot in the kitchen, then the inference is sound if you have had prior experience of like causes and effects. And if you predict that the plant food you bought from the garden shop in the winter will produce beautiful roses in the summer, your prediction will be accurate to the extent that there is ample evidence from your experience or the experience of others that this plant food has in the past had good results.

There are several ways that a posteriori analogical arguments can fail to adequately support a hypothesis. (1) We may not have enough similarities to support the declared strength of the analogy. Thus, Philo in DCNR points out that there are an insufficient number of similarities between the universe and human created artifacts. (2) There are so many differences between the things being compared that the analogy proportionally weakens the conclusion. Philo argues that the differences between natural and artificial objects are such that they cannot support any strong conclusions about a similarity in their origins (3) We may be so ignorant about the things being compared that the analogy between them is very weak. Philo points out how little we can claim to know about the universe itself to draw any credible analogies between the universe and artificial things created by humans. (4) There may be little or no relevance of the similarities put forth to support the desired conclusion. (5) Bias or partiality for the origin of one kind of thing (e.g. artifacts) should not be allowed to dictate conclusions about the origin of the thing to which it is being compared (e.g. the universe or natural objects therein). (6) The known origin of a part should not lead us to a conclusion about the origin of the whole of which it is a part.

16.2 Thought Experiments

Another tactic used by Hume in DCNR is the thought experiment, in which an imagined hypothetical situation is used to test a theory or principle. This tactic is used by Cleanthes in an attempt to bolster the Design Argument in such a way that it will avoid the criticisms of Philo. For example, Cleanthes imagines "an articulate voice" heard in the clouds by all people on earth who simultaneously understand the words being said. In a second thought experiment, Cleanthes imagines a library "peopled by natural volumes" first formed in the loins of an animal. In both cases, Cleanthes is attempting to show that there is sufficient resemblance between the imagined effects (for example, the articulate voice in the clouds and a voice we have heard in a dark room) to justify the conclusion that the causes must also resemble: an intelligent being.

16.3 Reductio ad Absurdum

Hume also uses the logical tactic of reductio ad absurdum to prove a point. The best examples are from the character Philo who shows Cleanthes and Demea that an infinite Deity is either willing to prevent evil, but is not sufficiently powerful to do this, or the Deity has the power to prevent evil, but is not willing to do so. If the Deity is both able and willing, "whence then is evil?"

Hume then reverses the argument by positing a finite God as the alleged designer of the world. His question is "What kind of God would we expect if the world we know was created from God's design?" By "the world we know" Hume means a world that is beset with natural and man-made disasters: earthquakes, floods, raging fires, crippling diseases, endless wars, and poverty. Hume contemplates that the kind of god who created such a world would probably mirror its own creation. It is highly likely that this deity is benevolent or intelligent (he might be a "stupid mechanic" who was attempting to copy the design of others). Moreover, there might be not one but several gods who created the world; they might have the human form, and the world might have been created as the result of procreation between these gods. All of these are very real possibilities if we ask the question "What kind of God or gods would design and oversee a world such as the world we now live in?" The answer (the reductio) is that it is not the kind of world that Christians and others would want to accept as part of their theology.

A version of the reductio ad absurdum argument is used in Hume's critique of those who are morally opposed to suicide. Hume begins by asking the opposer to consider the universal belief that "the almighty Creator has established general and immutable laws, by which all bodies, from the greatest planet to the smallest particle of matter, are maintained in their proper sphere and function" (On Suicide). He then presents the opposer with a choice between two alternatives: either suicide is a transgression of our duty to God or it is no transgression. If it is a transgression, then "in every case it is criminal to encroach upon [God's] laws and disturb their operation." But (Hume writes) "this seems absurd." Therefore, suicide is not a transgression of our duty to God. The person who commits suicide is lawfully employing "that power with which nature has endowed him."

16.4 Arguments A Priori

Arguments a priori ("abstract reasoning") are evaluated by rules that are quite different than the rules used to evaluate arguments a posteriori In his critique of Demea's argument for the existence and nature of God, Cleanthes claims that if we are to prove or demonstrate ("deduce") a conclusion by an argument a priori, then we must show that the contrary of the conclusion implies a contradiction. Consider the following time-worn syllogism:

1. Socrates is human
2. All humans are mortal
3. Therefore, Socrates is mortal

The contrary of (3) is "Socrates is not mortal." But this contradicts (1) and (2), which together form the proposition "Socrates is a mortal human." Another way to state this is to point out that (3) is contained in (1) and (2). We cannot distinctly conceive that Socrates is not mortal, given that we have previously hypothesized (1) and (2).

Notice that the validity of the argument has nothing to do with Socrates, other humans or being mortal. It has to do with the form of the argument. In this case, the form is (i) S is an h; (ii) All h's are m; (iii) Therefore S is an m. If we substitute "heifer" for the letter h, and "miserable" for the letter m, we get the valid argument: (a) Socrates is a heifer; (b) All heifers are misers; (c) Therefore, Socrates is a miser. It is the form of an argument a priori, not its content, that makes it valid or invalid.

But let's not lose sight of Hume's target. The target is not only Demea's argument for the "necessary existence" of God. It is the false assumption that one can prove matters of fact by arguments a priori. We see this assumption not only in arguments which attempt to prove the fact of God's existence, but also in metaphysical arguments attempting to prove the existence of an immaterial substance in the human body called "soul" and the related claim that there are immortal souls that now exist in an afterlife.

One of Hume's main contributions to philosophy is that no matter of fact can be proved by demonstration (that is, by an argument a priori). We cannot demonstrate that there are immortal souls any more than we can demonstrate that there are centaurs and griffins. The propositions "Souls do not exist," "God does not exist" and "Miracles do not exist" do not imply a contradiction because each of these propositions state something that is distinctly conceivable.

This does not mean that philosophers have nothing left to say about gods and souls. They can still do what contemporary philosophers call "conceptual analysis." They can analyze the concepts of "soul," "immortal," "afterlife," "God," and "miracle" in an attempt to clarify their essence or meaning. But these analyses, no matter how deep they go, can prove the *existence* of the objects or events to which these words refer. An analysis of the word "afterlife" can no more reveal the existence of an afterlife than an analysis of the word "frog" can reveal that frogs exist.

16.5 Arguments A Posteriori

How can we prove that frogs exist? Hume has already answered that question: by observation and experience. If I have identified something as a frog and heard it croak, then using the experimental principle, the next time I hear a sound that resembles the croaking sound I once heard, I can now infer the probable existence of a frog.

This is how all disputes about matters of fact are to be settled. Suppose that there is a terrible plane crash that kills hundreds of passengers save one, and the surviving passenger credits "the hand of God" for saving her life. If this explanation is disputed by others, we might be able to settle the dispute by asking whether there have been previous confirmable experiences of effects like this (surviving a plane crash) caused by the intervention of God. We might even want to go further and ask a follow-up question: "What would it be like to be saved by the hand of God? But this question would also have to be answered by reference to Hume's experimental principle.

The experimental principle also applies to claims about the existence of an afterlife. Suppose someone reports a near-death visual experience of their deceased grandmother. They insist that the experience was veridical, that is, they were seeing their real grandmother, not having a hallucination (perhaps caused by chemical and electrical discharges in the brain). They would argue that since their grandmother is physically dead, what they saw must have been their grandmother as she appears in an afterlife. Hume's approach to disputes like this is to ask whether the near-death visual experience resembles other experiences that are known to have been caused by events occurring in an afterlife. Are there any experiments that one can perform in the afterlife in which events are manipulated so as to cause veridical perceptions in this life? It is doubtful that there will be any volunteers for this job.

16.6 Summary

To summarize Hume's methodology with respect to the questions posed in DCNR and the essays on miracles and the immortality of the soul, Hume identifies the kind of argument being used and critically examines the argument using the relevant principles and rules. If the argument is a posteriori (inductive) and of the species analogical, then the experimental principle (like effects prove like causes) should be applied to determine the degree of probability (weak or strong) that we can plausibly attach to the conclusion.

> *It is certain that the liker the effects are which are seen and the liker the causes which are inferred, the stronger is the argument. Every departure on either side diminishes the probability and renders the experiment less conclusive* (DCNR, 34)..

VII APPENDICES

APPENDIX A

A. OF MIRACLES

From AN ENQUIRY CONCERNING HUMAN UNDERSTANDING
David Hume

I.

THERE is, in Dr. Tillotson's writings, an argument against the real presence, which is as concise, and elegant, and strong as any argument can possibly be supposed against a doctrine, so little worthy of a serious refutation. It is acknowledged on all hands, says that learned prelate, that the authority, either of the scripture or of tradition, is founded merely in the testimony of the apostles, who were eye-witnesses to those miracles of our Saviour, by which he proved his divine mission. Our evidence, then, for the truth of the Christian religion is less than the evidence for the truth of our senses; because, even in the first authors of our religion, it was no greater; and it is evident it must diminish in passing from them to their disciples; nor can any one rest such confidence in their testimony, as in the immediate object of his senses. But a weaker evidence can never destroy a stronger; and therefore, were the doctrine of the real presence ever so clearly revealed in scripture, it were directly contrary to the rules of just reasoning to give our assent to it. It contradicts sense, though both the scripture and tradition, on which it is supposed to be built, carry not such evidence with them as sense; when they are considered merely as external evidences, and are not brought home to every one's breast, by the immediate operation of the Holy Spirit.

Nothing is so convenient as a decisive argument of this kind, which must at least silence the most arrogant bigotry and superstition, and free us from their impertinent solicitations. I flatter myself, that I have discovered an argument of a like nature, which, if just, will, with the wise and learned, be an everlasting check to all kinds of superstitious delusion, and consequently, will be useful as long as the world endures. For so long, I presume, will the accounts of miracles and

Though experience be our only guide in reasoning concerning matters of fact; it must be acknowledged, that this guide is not altogether infallible, but in some cases is apt to lead us into errors. One, who in our climate, should expect better weather in any week of June than in one of December, would reason justly, and conformably to experience; but it is certain, that he may happen, in the event, to find himself mistaken. However, we may observe, that, in such a case, he would have no cause to complain of experience; because it commonly informs us beforehand of the uncertainty, by that contrariety of events, which we may learn from a diligent observation. All effects follow not with like certainty from their supposed causes. Some events are found, in all countries and all ages, to have been constantly conjoined together: Others are found to have been more variable, and sometimes to disappoint our expectations; so that, in our reasonings concerning matter of fact, there are all imaginable degrees of assurance, from the highest certainty to the lowest species of moral evidence.

A wise man, therefore, proportions his belief to the evidence. In such conclusions as are founded on an infallible experience, he expects the event with the last degree of assurance, and regards his past experience as a full proof of the future existence of that event. In other cases, he proceeds with more caution: He weighs the opposite experiments: He considers which side is supported by the greater number of experiments: To that side he inclines, with doubt and hesitation; and when at last he fixes his judgment, the evidence exceeds not what we properly call probability. All probability, then, supposes an opposition of experiments and observations, where the one side is found to overbalance the other, and to produce a degree of evidence, proportioned to the superiority. A hundred instances or experiments on one side, and fifty on another, afford a doubtful expectation of any event; though a hundred uniform experiments, with only one that is contradictory, reasonably beget a pretty strong degree of assurance. In all cases, we must balance the opposite experiments, where they are opposite, and deduct the smaller number from the greater, in order to know the exact force of the superior evidence.

To apply these principles to a particular instance; we may observe, that there is no species of reasoning more common, more useful, and even necessary to human life, than that which is derived from the testimony of men, and the reports of eye-witnesses and spectators. This species of reasoning, perhaps, one may deny to be founded on the relation of cause and effect. I shall not dispute about a word. It will be sufficient to observe, that our assurance in any argument of this kind is derived from no other principle than our observation of the veracity of human testimony, and of the usual conformity of facts to the reports of witnesses. It being a general maxim, that no objects have any discoverable connexion together, and that all the inferences, which we can draw from one to another, are founded merely on our experience of their constant and regular conjunction; it is evident, that we ought not to make an exception to this maxim in favour of human testimony, whose connexion with any event seems, in itself, as little necessary as any other. Were not the memory tenacious to a certain degree; had not men commonly an inclination to truth and a principle of probity; were they not sensible to shame, when detected in a falsehood: Were not these, I say, discovered by experience to be qualities, inherent in human nature, we should never repose the least confidence in human testimony. A man delirious, or noted for

And as the evidence, derived from witnesses and human testimony, is founded on past experience, so it varies with the experience, and is regarded either as a proof or a probability, according as the conjunction between any particular kind of report and any kind of object has been found to be constant or variable. There are a number of circumstances to be taken into consideration in all judgments of this kind;

and the ultimate standard, by which we determine all disputes, that may arise concerning them, is always derived from experience and observation. Where this experience is not entirely uniform on any side, it is attended with an unavoidable contrariety in our judgments, and with the same opposition and mutual destruction of argument as in every other kind of evidence. We frequently hesitate concerning the reports of others. We balance the opposite circumstances, which cause any doubt or uncertainty; and when we discover a superiority on any side, we incline to it; but still with a diminution of assurance, in proportion to the force of its antagonist.

This contrariety of evidence, in the present case, may be derived from several different causes; from the opposition of contrary testimony; from the character or number of the witnesses; from the manner of their delivering their testimony; or from the union of all these circumstances. We entertain a suspicion concerning any matter of fact, when the witnesses contradict each other; when they are but few, or of a doubtful character; when they have an interest in what they affirm; when they deliver their testimony with hesitation, or on the contrary, with too violent asseverations. There are many other particulars of the same kind, which may diminish or destroy the force of any argument, derived from human testimony.

Suppose, for instance, that the fact, which the testimony endeavours to establish, partakes of the extraordinary and the marvellous; in that case, the evidence, resulting from the testimony, admits of a diminution, greater or less, in proportion as the fact is more or less unusual. The reason, why we place any credit in witnesses and historians, is not derived from any connexion, which we perceive à priori, between testimony and reality, but because we are accustomed to find a conformity between them. But when the fact attested is such a one as has seldom fallen under our observation, here is a contest of two opposite experiences; of which the one destroys the other, as far as its force goes, and the superior can only operate on the mind by the force, which remains. The very same principle of experience, which gives us a certain degree of assurance in the testimony of witnesses, gives us also, in this case, another degree of assurance against the fact, which they endeavour to establish; from which contradiction there necessarily arises a counterpoize, and mutual destruction of belief and authority.

I should not believe such a story were it told me by Cato; was a proverbial saying in Rome, even during the lifetime of that philosophical patriot [21]. The incredibility of a fact, it was allowed, might invalidate so great an authority.

The Indian prince, who refused to believe the first relations concerning the effects of frost, reasoned justly; and it naturally required very strong testimony to engage his assent to facts, that arose from a state of nature, with which he was unacquainted, and which bore so little analogy to those events, of which he had had constant and uniform experience. Though they were not contrary to his experience, they were not conformable to it [22].

But in order to encrease the probability against the testimony of witnesses, let us suppose, that the fact, which they affirm, instead of being only marvellous, is really miraculous; and suppose also, that the testimony, considered apart and in itself, amounts to an entire proof; in that case, there is proof against proof, of which the strongest must prevail, but still with a diminution of its force, in proportion to that of its antagonist.

A miracle is a violation of the laws of nature; and as a firm and unalterable experience has established these laws, the proof against a miracle, from the very nature of the fact, is as entire as any argument from experience can possibly be imagined. Why is it more than probable, that all men must die; that lead cannot, of itself, remain suspended in the air; that fire consumes wood, and is extinguished by water; unless it be, that these events are found agreeable to the laws of nature, and there is required a violation of these laws, or in other words, a miracle to prevent them? Nothing is esteemed a miracle, if it ever happen in the common course of nature. It is no miracle that a man, seemingly in good health, should die on a sudden: because such a kind of death, though more unusual than any other, has yet been frequently observed to happen. But it is a miracle, that a dead man should come to life; because that has never been observed, in any age or country. There must, therefore, be a uniform experience against every miraculous event, otherwise the event would not merit that appellation. And as an uniform experience amounts to a proof, there is here a direct and full proof, from the nature of the fact, against the existence of any miracle; nor can such a proof be destroyed, or the miracle rendered credible, but by an opposite proof, which is superior [23].

The plain consequence is (and it is a general maxim worthy of our attention), That no testimony is sufficient to establish a miracle, unless the testimony be of such a kind, that its falsehood would be more miraculous, than the fact, which it endeavours to establish: And even in that case there is a mutual destruction of arguments, and the superior only gives us an assurance suitable to that degree of force, which remains, after deducting the inferior. When anyone tells me, that he saw a dead man restored to life, I immediately consider with myself, whether it be more probable, that this person should either deceive or be deceived, or that the fact, which he relates, should really have happened. I weigh the one miracle against the other; and according to the superiority, which I discover, I pronounce my decision, and always reject the greater miracle. If the falsehood of his testimony would be more miraculous, than the event which he relates; then, and not till then, can he pretend to command my belief or opinion.

II.

In the foregoing reasoning we have supposed, that the testimony, upon which a miracle is founded, may possibly amount to an entire proof, and that the falsehood of that testimony would be a real prodigy: But it is easy to shew, that we have been a great deal too liberal in our concession, and that there never was a miraculous event established on so full an evidence.

For first, there is not to be found, in all history, any miracle attested by a sufficient number of men, of such unquestioned good-sense, education, and learning, as to secure us against all delusion in themselves; of such undoubted integrity, as to place them beyond all suspicion of any design to deceive others; of such credit and reputation in the eyes of mankind, as to have a great deal to lose in case of their being detected in any falsehood; and at the same time, attesting facts, performed in such a public manner, and in so celebrated a part of the world, as to render the detection unavoidable: All which circumstances are requisite to give us a full assurance in the testimony of men.

Secondly. We may observe in human nature a principle, which, if strictly examined, will be found to diminish extremely the assurance, which we might, from human testimony, have, in any kind of prodigy. The maxim, by which we commonly conduct ourselves in our reasonings, is, that the objects, of which we have no experience, resemble those, of which we have; that what we have found to be most usual is always most probable; and that where there is an opposition of arguments, we ought to give the preference to such as are founded on the greatest number of past observations. But though, in proceeding by this rule, we readily reject any fact which is unusual and incredible in an ordinary degree; yet in advancing farther, the mind observes not always the same rule; but when anything is affirmed utterly absurd and miraculous, it rather the more readily admits of such a fact, upon account of that very circumstance, which ought to destroy all its authority. The passion of surprize and wonder, arising from miracles, being an agreeable emotion, gives a sensible tendency towards the belief of those events, from which it is derived. And this goes so far, that even those who cannot enjoy this pleasure immediately, nor can believe those miraculous events, of which they are informed, yet love to partake of the satisfaction at second-hand or by rebound, and place a pride and delight in exciting the admiration of others.

With what greediness are the miraculous accounts of travellers received, their descriptions of sea and land monsters, their relations of wonderful adventures, strange men, and uncouth manners? But if the spirit of religion join itself to the love of wonder, there is an end of common sense; and human testimony, in these circumstances, loses all pretensions to authority. A religionist may be an enthusiast, and imagine he sees what has no reality: He may know his narrative to be false, and yet persevere in it, with the best intentions in the world, for the sake of promoting so holy a cause: Or even where this delusion has not place, vanity, excited by so strong a temptation, operates on him more powerfully than on the rest of mankind in any other circumstances; and self-interest with equal force. His auditors may not have, and commonly have not, sufficient judgment to canvass his evidence: What judgment they have, they renounce by principle, in these sublime and mysterious subjects: Or if they were ever so willing to employ it, passion and a heated imagination disturb the regularity of its operations. Their credulity encreases his impudence: And his impudence overpowers their credulity.

Eloquence, when at its highest pitch, leaves little room for reason or reflection; but addressing itself entirely to the fancy or the affections, captivates the willing hearers, and subdues their understanding. Happily, this pitch it seldom attains. But what a Tully or a Demosthenes could scarcely effect over a Roman or Athenian audience, every Capuchin, every itinerant or stationary teacher can perform over the generality of mankind, and in a higher degree, by touching such gross and vulgar passions.

The many instances of forged miracles, and prophecies, and supernatural events, which, in all ages, have either been detected by contrary evidence, or which detect themselves by their absurdity, prove sufficiently the strong propensity of mankind to the extraordinary and the marvellous, and ought reasonably to beget a suspicion against all relations of this kind. This is our natural way of thinking, even with regard to the most common and most credible events. For instance: There is no kind of report, which rises so easily, and spreads so quickly, especially in country places and provincial towns, as those concerning marriages; insomuch that two young persons of equal condition never see each other twice, but the whole neighbourhood immediately join them together. The pleasure of telling a piece of news so interesting, of propagating it, and of being the first reporters of it, spreads the intelligence. And this is so well known, that no man of sense gives attention to these reports, till he finds them confirmed by some greater evidence. Do not the same passions, and others still stronger, incline the generality of mankind to believe and report, with the greatest vehemence and assurance, all religious miracles?

Thirdly. It forms a strong presumption against all supernatural and miraculous relations, that they are observed chiefly to abound among ignorant and barbarous nations; or if a civilized people has ever given admission to any of them, that people will be found to have received them from ignorant and barbarous ancestors, who transmitted them with that inviolable sanction and authority, which always attend received opinions. When we peruse the first histories of all nations, we are apt to imagine ourselves transported into some new world; where the whole frame of nature is disjointed, and every element performs its operations in a different manner, from what it does at present. Battles, revolutions, pestilence, famine, and death are never the effect of those natural causes, which we experience. Prodigies, omens, oracles, judgments, quite obscure the few natural events, that are intermingled with them. But as the former grow thinner every page, in proportion as we advance nearer the enlightened ages, we soon learn, that there is nothing mysterious or supernatural in the case, but that all proceeds from the usual propensity of mankind towards the marvellous, and that, though this inclination may at intervals receive a check from sense and learning, it can never be thoroughly extirpated from human nature.

It is strange, a judicious reader is apt to say, upon the perusal of these wonderful historians, that such prodigious events never happen in our days. But it is nothing strange, I hope, that men should lie in all ages. You must surely have seen instances enow of that frailty. You have yourself heard many such marvellous relations started, which, being treated with scorn by all the wise and judicious, have at last been abandoned even by the vulgar. Be assured, that those renowned lies, which have spread and flourished to such a monstrous height, arose from like beginnings; but being sown in a more proper soil, shot up at last into prodigies almost equal to those which they relate.

It was a wise policy in that false prophet, Alexander, who, though now forgotten, was once so famous, to lay the first scene of his impostures in Paphlagonia, where, as Lucian tells us, the people were extremely ignorant and stupid, and ready to swallow even the grossest delusion. People at a distance, who are weak enough to think the matter at all worth enquiry, have no opportunity of receiving better information. The stories come magnified to them by a hundred circumstances. Fools are industrious in propagating the imposture; while the wise and learned are contented, in general, to deride its absurdity, without informing themselves of the particular facts, by which it may be distinctly refuted. And thus the impostor above-mentioned was enabled to proceed, from his ignorant Paphlagonians, to the enlisting of votaries, even among the Grecian philosophers, and men of the most eminent rank and distinction in Rome: Nay, could engage the attention of that sage emperor Marcus Aurelius; so far as to make him trust the success of a military expedition to his delusive prophecies.

The advantages are so great, of starting an imposture among an ignorant people, that, even though the delusion should be too gross to impose on the generality of them (which, though seldom, is sometimes the case) it has a much better chance for succeeding in remote countries, than if the first scene had been laid in a city renowned for arts and knowledge. The most ignorant and barbarous of these barbarians carry the report abroad. None of their countrymen have a large correspondence, or sufficient credit and authority to contradict and beat down the delusion. Men's inclination to the marvellous has full opportunity to display itself. And thus a story, which is universally exploded in the place where it was first started, shall pass for certain at a thousand miles distance. But had Alexander fixed his residence at Athens, the philosophers of that renowned mart of learning had immediately spread, throughout the whole Roman empire, their sense of the matter; which, being supported by so great authority, and displayed by all the force of reason and eloquence, had entirely opened the eyes of mankind. It is true; Lucian, passing by chance through Paphlagonia, had an opportunity of performing this good office. But, though much to be wished, it does not always happen, that every Alexander meets with a Lucian, ready to expose and detect his impostures.

I may add as a fourth reason, which diminishes the authority of prodigies, that there is no testimony for any, even those which have not been expressly detected, that is not opposed by an infinite number of witnesses; so that not only the miracle destroys the credit of testimony, but the testimony destroys itself. To make this the better understood, let us consider, that, in matters of religion, whatever is different is contrary; and that it is impossible the religions of ancient Rome, of Turkey, of Siam, and of China should, all of them, be established on any solid foundation. Every miracle, therefore, pretended to have been wrought in any of these religions (and all of them abound in miracles), as its direct scope is to establish the particular system to which it is attributed; so has it the same force, though more indirectly, to overthrow every other system. In destroying a rival system, it likewise destroys the credit of those miracles, on which that system was established; so that all the prodigies of different religions are to be regarded as contrary facts, and the evidences of these prodigies, whether weak or strong, as opposite to each other. According to this method of reasoning, when we believe any miracle of Mahomet or his successors, we have for our warrant the testimony of a few barbarous Arabians: And on the other hand, we are to regard the authority of Titus Livius, Plutarch, Tacitus, and, in short, of all the authors and witnesses, Grecian, Chinese, and Roman Catholic, who have related any miracle in their particular religion; I say, we are to regard their testimony in the same light as if they had mentioned that Mahometan miracle, and had in express terms contradicted it, with the same certainty as they have for the miracle they relate. This argument may appear over subtile and refined; but is not in reality different from the reasoning of a judge, who supposes, that the credit of two witnesses, maintaining a crime against any one, is destroyed by the testimony of two others, who affirm him to have been two hundred leagues distant, at the same instant when the crime is said to have been committed.

One of the best attested miracles in all profane history, is that which Tacitus reports of Vespasian, who cured a blind man in Alexandria, by means of his spittle, and a lame man by the mere touch of his foot; in obedience to a vision of the god Serapis, who had enjoined them to have recourse to the Emperor, for these miraculous cures. The story may be seen in that fine historian [24]; where every circumstance seems to add weight to the testimony, and might be displayed at large with all the force of argument and eloquence, if any one were now concerned to enforce the evidence of that exploded and idolatrous superstition. The gravity, solidity, age, and probity of so great an emperor, who, through the whole course of his life, conversed in a familiar manner with his friends and courtiers, and never affected those extraordinary airs of divinity assumed by Alexander and Demetrius. The historian, a contemporary writer, noted for candour and veracity, and withal, the greatest and most penetrating genius, perhaps, of all antiquity; and so free from any tendency to credulity, that he even lies under the contrary imputation, of atheism and profaneness: The persons, from whose authority he related the miracle, of established character for judgment and veracity, as we may well presume; eye-witnesses of the fact, and confirming their testimony, after the Flavian family was despoiled of the empire, and could no longer give any reward, as the price of a lie. Utrumque, qui interfuere, nunc quoque memorant, postquam nullum mendacio pretium. To which if we add the public nature of the facts, as related, it will appear, that no evidence can well be supposed stronger for so gross and so palpable a falsehood.

There is also a memorable story related by Cardinal De Retz, which may well deserve our consideration. When that intriguing politician fled into Spain, to avoid the persecution of his enemies, he passed through Saragossa, the capital of Arragon, where he was shewn, in the cathedral, a man, who had served seven years as a doorkeeper, and was well known to everybody in town, that had ever paid his devotions at that church. He had been seen, for so long a time, wanting a leg; but recovered that limb by the rubbing of holy oil upon the stump; and the cardinal assures us that he saw him with two legs. This miracle was vouched by all the canons of the church; and the whole company in town were appealed to for a confirmation of the fact; whom the cardinal found, by their zealous devotion, to be thorough believers of the miracle. Here the relater was also cotemporary to the supposed prodigy, of an incredulous and libertine character, as well as of great genius; the miracle of so singular a nature as could scarcely admit of a counterfeit, and the witnesses very numerous, and all of them, in a manner, spectators of the fact, to which they gave their testimony. And what adds mightily to the force of the evidence, and may double our surprize on this occasion, is, that the cardinal himself, who relates the story, seems not to give any credit to it, and consequently cannot be suspected of any concurrence in the holy fraud. He considered justly, that it was not requisite, in order to reject a fact of this nature, to be able accurately to disprove the testimony, and to trace its falsehood, through all the circumstances of knavery and credulity which produced it. He knew, that, as this was commonly altogether impossible at any small distance of time and place; so was it extremely difficult, even where one was immediately present, by reason of the bigotry, ignorance, cunning, and roguery of a great part of mankind. He therefore concluded, like a just reasoner, that such an evidence carried falsehood upon the very face of it, and that a miracle, supported by any human testimony, was more properly a subject of derision than of argument.

There surely never was a greater number of miracles ascribed to one person, than those, which were lately said to have been wrought in France upon the tomb of Abbé Paris, the famous Jansenist, with whose sanctity the people were so long deluded. The curing of the sick, giving hearing to the deaf, and sight to the blind, were everywhere talked of as the usual effects of that holy sepulchre. But what is more extraordinary; many of the miracles were immediately proved upon the spot, before judges of unquestioned integrity, attested by witnesses of credit and distinction, in a learned age, and on the most eminent theatre that is now in the world. Nor is this all: A relation of them was published and dispersed everywhere; nor were the Jesuits, though a learned body, supported by the civil magistrate, and determined enemies to those opinions, in whose favour the miracles were said to have been wrought, ever able distinctly to refute or detect them[25]. Where shall we find such a number of circumstances, agreeing to the corroboration of one fact? And what have we to oppose to such a cloud of witnesses, but the absolute impossibility or miraculous nature of the events, which they relate? And this surely, in the eyes of all reasonable people, will alone be regarded as a sufficient refutation.

Is the consequence just, because some human testimony has the utmost force and authority in some cases, when it relates the battle of Philippi or Pharsalia for instance; that therefore all kinds of testimony must, in all cases, have equal force and authority? Suppose that the Cæsarean and Pompeian factions had, each of them, claimed the victory in these battles, and that the historians of each party had uniformly ascribed the advantage to their own side; how could mankind, at this distance, have been able to determine between them? The contrariety is equally strong between the miracles related by Herodotus or Plutarch, and those delivered by Mariana, Bede, or any monkish historian.

The wise lend a very academic faith to every report which favours the passion of the reporter; whether it magnifies his country, his family, or himself, or in any other way strikes in with his natural inclinations and propensities. But what greater temptation than to appear a missionary, a prophet, an ambassador from heaven? Who would not encounter many dangers and difficulties, in order to attain so sublime a character? Or if, by the help of vanity and a heated imagination, a man has first made a convert of himself, and entered seriously into the delusion; whoever scruples to make use of pious frauds, in support of so holy and meritorious a cause?

The smallest spark may here kindle into the greatest flame; because the materials are always prepared for it. The avidum genus auricularum [26], the gazing populace, receive greedily, without examination, whatever sooths superstition, and promotes wonder.

How many stories of this nature have, in all ages, been detected and exploded in their infancy? How many more have been celebrated for a time, and have afterwards sunk into neglect and oblivion? Where such reports, therefore, fly about, the solution of the phænomenon is obvious; and we judge in conformity to regular experience and observation, when we account for it by the known and natural principles of credulity and delusion. And shall we, rather than have a recourse to so natural a solution, allow of a miraculous violation of the most established laws of nature?

I need not mention the difficulty of detecting a falsehood in any private or even public history, at the place, where it is said to happen; much more when the scene is removed to ever so small a distance. Even a court of judicature, with all the authority, accuracy, and judgment, which they can employ, find themselves often at a loss to distinguish between truth and falsehood in the most recent actions. But the matter never comes to any issue, if trusted to the common method of altercation and debate and flying rumours; especially when men's passions have taken part on either side.

In the infancy of new religions, the wise and learned commonly esteem the matter too inconsiderable to deserve their attention or regard. And when afterwards they would willingly detect the cheat, in order to undeceive the deluded multitude, the season is now past, and the records and witnesses, which might clear up the matter, have perished beyond recovery.

No means of detection remain, but those which must be drawn from the very testimony itself of the reporters: And these, though always sufficient with the judicious and knowing, are commonly too fine to fall under the comprehension of the vulgar.

Upon the whole, then, it appears, that no testimony for any kind of miracle has ever amounted to a probability, much less to a proof; and that, even supposing it amounted to a proof, it would be opposed by another proof; derived from the very nature of the fact, which it would endeavour to establish. It is experience only, which gives authority to human testimony; and it is the same experience, which assures us of the laws of nature. When, therefore, these two kinds of experience are contrary, we have nothing to do but substract the one from the other, and embrace an opinion, either on one side or the other, with that assurance which arises from the remainder. But according to the principle here explained, this substraction, with regard to all popular religions, amounts to an entire annihilation; and therefore we may establish it as a maxim, that no human testimony can have such force as to prove a miracle, and make it a just foundation for any such system of religion.

I beg the limitations here made may be remarked, when I say, that a miracle can never be proved, so as to be the foundation of a system of religion. For I own, that otherwise, there may possibly be miracles, or violations of the usual course of nature, of such a kind as to admit of proof from human testimony; though, perhaps, it will be impossible to find any such in all the records of history. Thus, suppose, all authors, in all languages, agree, that, from the first of January 1600, there was a total darkness over the whole earth for eight days: Suppose that the tradition of this extraordinary event is still strong and lively among the people: That all travellers, who return from foreign countries, bring us accounts of the same tradition, without the least variation or contradiction: It is evident, that our present philosophers, instead of doubting the fact, ought to receive it as certain, and ought to search for the causes whence it might be derived. The decay, corruption, and dissolution of nature is an event rendered probable by so many analogies, that any phænomenon, which seems to have a tendency towards that catastrophe, comes within the reach of human testimony, if that testimony be very extensive and uniform.

But suppose, that all the historians who treat of England, should agree, that, on the first of January 1600, Queen Elizabeth died; that both before and after her death she was seen by her physicians and the whole court, as is usual with persons of her rank; that her successor was acknowledged and proclaimed by the parliament; and that, after being interred a month, she again appeared, resumed the throne, and governed England for three years: I must confess that I should be surprized at the concurrence of so many odd circumstances, but should not have the least inclination to believe so miraculous an event. I should not doubt of her pretended death, and of those other public circumstances that followed it: I should only assert it to have been pretended, and that it neither was, nor possibly could be real. You would in vain object to me the difficulty, and almost impossibility of deceiving the world in an affair of such consequence; the wisdom and solid judgment of that renowned queen; with the little or no advantage which she could reap from so poor an artifice: All this might astonish me; but I would still reply, that the knavery and folly of men are such common phænomena, that I should rather believe the most extraordinary events to arise from their concurrence, than admit of so signal a violation of the laws of nature.

But should this miracle be ascribed to any new system of religion; men, in all ages, have been so much imposed on by ridiculous stories of that kind, that this very circumstance would be a full proof of a cheat, and sufficient, with all men of sense, not only to make them reject the fact, but even reject it without farther examination. Though the Being to whom the miracle is ascribed, be, in this case, Almighty, it does not, upon that account, become a whit more probable; since it is impossible for us to know the attributes or actions of such a Being, otherwise than from the experience which we have of his productions, in the usual course of nature. This still reduces us to past observation, and obliges us to compare the instances of the violation of truth in the testimony of men, with those of the violation of the laws of nature by miracles, in order to judge which of them is most likely and probable. As the violations of truth are more common in the testimony concerning religious miracles, than in that concerning any other matter of fact; this must diminish very much the authority of the former testimony, and make us form a general resolution, never to lend any attention to it, with whatever specious pretence it may be covered.

Lord Bacon seems to have embraced the same principles of reasoning. We ought, says he, to make a collection or particular history of all monsters and prodigious births or productions, and in a word of everything new, rare, and extraordinary in nature. But this must be done with the most severe scrutiny, lest we depart from truth. Above all, every relation must be considered as suspicious, which depends in any degree upon religion, as the prodigies of Livy: And no less so, everything that is to be found in the writers of natural magic or alchimy, or such authors, who seem, all of them, to have an unconquerable appetite for falsehood and fable[27].

I am the better pleased with the method of reasoning here delivered, as I think it may serve to confound those dangerous friends or disguised enemies to the Christian Religion, who have undertaken to defend it by the principles of human reason. Our most holy religion is founded on Faith, not on reason; and it is a sure method of exposing it to put it to such a trial as it is, by no means, fitted to endure. To make this more evident, let us examine those miracles, related in scripture; and not to lose ourselves in too wide a field, let us confine ourselves to such as we find in the Pentateuch, which we shall examine, according to the principles of these pretended Christians, not as the word or testimony of God himself, but as the production of a mere human writer and historian. Here then we are first to consider a book, presented to us by a barbarous and ignorant people, written in an age when they were still more barbarous, and in all probability long after the facts which it relates, corroborated by no concurring testimony, and resembling those fabulous accounts, which every nation gives of its origin. Upon reading this book, we find it full of prodigies and miracles. It gives an account of a state of the world and of human nature entirely different from the present: Of our fall from that state: Of the age of man, extended to near a thousand years: Of the destruction of the world by a deluge: Of the arbitrary choice of one people, as the favourites of heaven; and that people the countrymen of the author: Of their deliverance from bondage by prodigies the most astonishing imaginable: I desire any one to lay his hand upon his heart, and after a serious consideration declare, whether he thinks that the falsehood of such a book, supported by such a testimony, would be more extraordinary and miraculous than all the miracles it relates; which is, however, necessary to make it be received, according to the measures of probability above established.

What we have said of miracles may be applied, without any variation, to prophecies; and indeed, all prophecies are real miracles, and as such only, can be admitted as proofs of any revelation. If it did not exceed the capacity of human nature to foretel future events, it would be absurd to employ any prophecy as an argument for a divine mission or authority from heaven. So that, upon the whole, we may conclude, that the Christian Religion not only was at first attended with miracles, but even at this day cannot be believed by any reasonable person without one. Mere reason is insufficient to convince us of its veracity: And whoever is moved by Faith to assent to it, is conscious of a continued miracle in his own person, which subverts all the principles of his understanding, and gives him a determination to believe what is most contrary to custom and experience.

---

21. Plutarch, in vita Catonis.

22. See NOTE [I].
NO INDIAN, it is evident, could have experience that water did not freeze in cold climates. This is placing nature in a situation quite unknown to him; and it is impossible for him to tell à priori what will result from it. It is making a new experiment, the consequence of which is always uncertain. One may sometimes conjecture from analogy what will follow; but still this is but conjecture. And it must be confessed, that, in the present case of freezing, the event follows contrary to the rules of analogy, and is such as a rational Indian would not look for. The operations of cold upon water are not gradual, according to the degrees of cold; but whenever it comes to the freezing point, the water passes in a moment, from the utmost liquidity to perfect hardness. Such an event, therefore, may be denominated extraordinary, and requires a pretty strong testimony, to render it credible to people in a warm climate: But still it is not miraculous, nor contrary to uniform experience of the course of nature in cases where all the circumstances are the same. The inhabitants of Sumatra have always seen water fluid in their own climate, and the freezing of their rivers ought to be deemed a prodigy: But they never saw water in Muscovy during the winter; and therefore they cannot reasonably be positive what would there be the consequence.

23. See NOTE [K].
SOMETIMES an event may not, in itself, seem to be contrary to the laws of nature, and yet, if it were real, it might, by reason of some circumstances, be denominated a miracle; because, in fact, it is contrary to these laws. Thus if a person, claiming a divine authority, should command a sick person to be well, a healthful man to fall down dead,

the clouds to pour rain, the winds to blow, in short, should order many natural events, which immediately follow upon his command; these might justly be esteemed miracles, because they are really, in this case, contrary to the laws of nature. For if any suspicion remains, that the event and command concurred by accident, there is no miracle and no transgression of the laws of nature. If this suspicion be removed, there is evidently a miracle, and a transgression of these laws; because nothing can be more contrary to nature than that the voice or command of a man should have such an influence. A miracle may be accurately defined, a transgression of a law of nature by a particular volition of the Deity, or by the interposition of some invisible agent. A miracle may either be discoverable by men or not. This alters not its nature and essence. The raising of a house or ship into the air is a visible miracle. The raising of a feather, when the wind wants ever so little of a force requisite for that purpose, is as real a miracle, though not so sensible with regard to us.

24. Hist. lib. v. cap. 8. Suetonius gives nearly the same account in vita Vesp.

25. See NOTE [L].

THIS book was writ by Mons. Montgeron, counsellor or judge of the parliament of Paris, a man of figure and character, who was also a martyr to the cause, and is now said to be somewhere in a

There is another book in three volumes (called Recueil des Miracles de l'Abbé Paris) giving an account of many of these miracles, and accompanied with prefatory discourses, which are very well written. There runs, however, through the whole of these a ridiculous comparison between the miracles of our Saviour and those of the Abbé; wherein it is asserted, that the evidence for the latter is equal to that for the former: As if the testimony of men could ever be put in the balance with that of God himself, who conducted the pen of the inspired writers. If these writers, indeed, were to be considered merely as human testimony, the French author is very moderate in his comparison; since he might, with some appearance of reason, pretend, that the Jansenist miracles much surpass the other in evidence and authority. The following circumstances are drawn from authentic papers, inserted in the above-mentioned book.

Many of the miracles of Abbé Paris were proved immediately by witnesses before the officiality or bishop's court at Paris, under the eye of cardinal Noailles, whose character for integrity and capacity was never contested even by his enemies.

His successor in the archbishopric was an enemy to the Jansenists, and for that reason promoted to the see by the court. Yet 22 rectors or cures of Paris, with infinite earnestness, press him to examine those miracles, which they assert to be known to the whole world, and undisputably certain: But he wisely forbore.

The Molinist party had tried to discredit these miracles in one instance, that of Mademoiselle le Franc. But, besides that their proceedings were in many respects the most irregular in the world, particularly in citing only a few of the Jansenist witnesses, whom they tampered with: Besides this, I say, they soon found themselves overwhelmed by a cloud of new witnesses, one hundred and twenty in number, most of them persons of credit and substance in Paris, who gave oath for the miracle. This was accompanied with a solemn and earnest appeal to the parliament. But the parliament were forbidden by authority to meddle in the affair. It was at last observed, that where men are heated by zeal and enthusiasm, there is no degree of human testimony so strong as may not be procured for the greatest absurdity: And those who will be so silly as to examine the affair by that medium, and seek particular flaws in the testimony, are almost sure to be confounded. It must be a miserable imposture, indeed, that does not prevail in that contest.

All who have been in France about that time have heard of the reputation of Mons. Heraut, the lieutenant de Police, whose vigilance, penetration, activity, and extensive intelligence have been much talked of. This magistrate, who by the nature of his office is almost absolute, was invested with full powers, on purpose to suppress or discredit these miracles; and he frequently seized immediately, and examined the witnesses and subjects of them: But never could reach any thing satisfactory against them.

In the case of Mademoiselle Thibaut he sent the famous De Sylva to examine her; whose evidence is very curious. The physician declares, that it was impossible she could have been so ill as was proved by witnesses; because it was impossible, she could, in so short a time, have recovered so perfectly as he found her. He reasoned, like a man of sense, from natural causes; but the opposite party told him, that the whole was a miracle, and that his evidence was the very best proof of it.

The Molinists were in a sad dilemma. They durst not assert the absolute insufficiency of human evidence, to prove a miracle. They were obliged to say, that these miracles were wrought by witchcraft and the devil. But they were told, that this was the resource of the Jews of old.

No Jansenist was ever embarrassed to account for the cessation of the miracles, when the churchyard was shut up by the king's edict. It was the touch of the tomb, which produced these extraordinary effects; and when no one could approach the tomb, no effects could be expected. God, indeed, could have thrown down the walls in a moment; but he is master of his own graces and works, and it belongs not to us to account for them. He did not throw down the walls of every city like those of Jericho, on the sounding of the rams' horns, nor break up the prison of every apostle, like that of St. Paul.

No less a man, than the Duc de Chatillon, a duke and peer of France, of the highest rank and family, gives evidence of a miraculous cure, performed upon a servant of his, who had lived several years in his house with a visible and palpable infirmity.

I shall conclude with observing, that no clergy are more celebrated for strictness of life and manners than the secular clergy of France, particularly the rectors or curés of Paris, who bear testimony to these impostures.

The learning, genius, and probity of the gentlemen, and the austerity of the nuns of Port-Royal, have been much celebrated all over Europe. Yet they all give evidence for a miracle, wrought on the niece of the famous Pascal, whose sanctity of life, as well as extraordinary capacity, is well known. The famous Racine gives an account of this miracle in his famous history of Port Royal, and fortifies it with all the proofs, which a multitude of nuns, priests, physicians, and men of the world, all of them of undoubted credit, could bestow upon it. Several men of letters, particularly the bishop of Tournay, thought this miracle so certain, as to employ it in the refutation of atheists and freethinkers. The queen-regent of France, who was extremely prejudiced against the Port-Royal, send her own physician to examine the miracle, who returned an absolute convert. In short, the supernatural cure was so uncontestable, that it saved, for a time, that famous monastery from the ruin with which it was threatened by the Jesuits. Had it been a cheat, it had certainly been detected by such sagacious and powerful antagonists, and must have hastened the ruin of the contrivers. Our divines, who can build up a formidable castle from such despicable materials; what a prodigious fabric could they have reared from these and many other circumstances, which I have not mentioned! How often would the great names of Pascal, Racine, Arnaud, Nicole, have resounded in our ears? But if they be wise, they had better adopt the miracle, as being more worth, a thousand times, than all the rest of their collection. Besides, it may serve very much to their purpose. For that miracle was really performed by the touch of an authentic holy prickle of the holy thorn, which composed the holy crown, which, &c.

26. Lucret.E

27. Nov. Org. lib. ii. aph. 29..

APPENDIX B

B. OF THE IMMORTALITY OF THE SOUL

David Hume
Posthumous Publication

BY the mere light of reason it seems difficult to prove the Immortality of the Soul. The arguments for it are commonly derived either from metaphysical topics, or moral or physical. But in reality, it is the gospel, and the gospel alone, that has brought life and immortality to light.

I. Metaphysical topics are founded on the supposition that the soul is immaterial, and that it is impossible for thought to belong to a material substance.

But just metaphysics teach us, that the notion of substance is wholly confused and imperfect, and that we have no other idea of any substance than as an aggregate of particular qualities, inhering in an unknown something. Matter, therefore, and spirit are at bottom equally unknown; and we cannot determine what qualities may inhere in the one or in the other.

They likewise teach us, that nothing can be decided a priori concerning any cause or effect; and that experience being the only source of our judgments of this nature, we cannot know from any other principle, whether matter, by its structure or arrangement, may not be the cause of thought. Abstract reasonings cannot decide any question of fact or existence.

But admitting a spiritual substance to be dispersed throughout the universe, like the etherial fire of the Stoics, and to be the only inherent subject of thought; we have reason to conclude from analogy, that nature uses it after the same manner she does the other substance, matter. She employs it as a kind of paste or clay; modifies it into a variety of forms and existences; dissolves after a time each modification; and from its substance erects a new form. As the same material substance may successively compose the body of all animals, the same spiritual substance may compose their minds: Their consciousness, or that system of thought, which they formed during life, may be continually dissolved by death; and nothing interest them in the new modification. The most positive asserters of the mortality of the soul, never denied the immortality of its substance. And that an immaterial substance, as well as a material, may lose its memory or consciousness appears, in part, from experience, if the soul be immaterial.

Reasoning from the common course of nature, and without supposing any new interposition of the supreme cause, which ought always to be excluded from philosophy; what is incorruptible must also be ingenerable. The soul, therefore, if immortal, existed before our birth: And if the former state of existence no wise concerned us, neither will the latter.

Animals undoubtedly feel, think, love, hate, will, and even reason, tho' in a more imperfect manner than man. Are their souls also immaterial and immortal?

II. Let us now consider the moral arguments, chiefly those arguments derived from the justice of God, which is supposed to be farther interested in the farther punishment of the vicious, and reward of the virtuous.

But these arguments are grounded on the supposition, that God has attributes beyond what he has exerted in this universe, with which alone we are acquainted. Whence do we infer the existence of these attributes?

It is very safe for us to affirm, that, whatever we know the deity to have actually done, is best; but it is very dangerous to affirm, that he must always do what to us seems best. In how many instances would this reasoning fail us with regard to the present world?

But if any purpose of nature be clear, we may affirm, that the whole scope and intention of man's creation, so far as we can judge by natural reason, is limited to the present life. With how weak a concern, from the original, inherent structure of the mind and passions, does he ever look farther? What comparison, either for steddiness or efficacy, between so floating an idea, and the most doubtful persuasion of any matter of fact, that occurs in common life.

There arise, indeed, in some minds, some unaccountable terrors with regard to futurity: But these would quickly vanish, were they not artificially fostered by precept and education. And those, who foster them; what is their motive? Only to gain a livelihood, and to acquire power and riches in this world. Their very zeal and industry, therefore, are an argument against them.

What cruelty, what iniquity, what injustice in nature, to confine thus all our concern, as well as all our knowledge, to the present life, if there be another scene still awaiting us, of infinitely greater consequence? Ought this barbarous deceit to be ascribed to a beneficent and wise being?

Observe with what exact proportion the task to be performed and the performing powers are adjusted throughout all nature. If the reason of man gives him a great superiority above other animals, his necessities are proportionably multiplied upon him. His whole time, his whole capacity, activity, courage, passion, find sufficient employment, in fencing against the miseries of his present condition. And frequently, nay almost always, are too slender for the business assigned them.

A pair of shoes, perhaps, was never yet wrought to the highest degree of perfection, which that commodity is capable of attaining. Yet is it necessary, at least very useful, that there should be some politicians and moralists, even some geometers, historians, poets, and philosophers among mankind.

The powers of men are no more superior to their wants, considered merely in this life, than those of foxes and hares are, compared to their wants and to their period of existence. The inference from parity of reason is therefore obvious.

On the theory of the soul's mortality, the inferiority of women's capacity is easily accounted for: Their domestic life requires no higher faculties either of mind or body. This circumstance vanishes and becomes absolutely insignificant, on the religious theory: The one sex has an equal task to perform with the other: Their powers of reason and resolution ought also to have been equal, and both of them infinitely greater than at present.

As every effect implies a cause, and that another, till we reach the first cause of all, which is the Deity; everything, that happens, is ordained by him; and nothing can be the object of his punishment or vengeance.

By what rule are punishments and rewards distributed? What is the divine standard of merit and demerit? Shall we suppose, that human sentiments have place in the deity? However bold that hypothesis, we have no conception of any other sentiments.

According to human sentiments, sense, courage, good manners, industry, prudence, genius, &c. are essential parts of personal merit. Shall we therefore erect an elysium for poets and heroes, like that of the antient mythology? Why confine all rewards to one species of virtue?

Punishment, without any proper end or purpose, is inconsistent with our ideas of goodness and justice; and no end can be served by it after the whole scene is closed.

Punishment, according to our conceptions, should bear some proportion to the offence. Why then eternal punishment for the temporary offences of so frail a creature as man? Can any one approve of Alexander's rage, who intended to exterminate a whole nation, because they had seized his favourite horse, Bucephalus?

Heaven and hell suppose two distinct species of men, the good and the bad. But the greatest part of mankind float between vice and virtue.

Were one to go round the world with an intention of giving a good supper to the righteous and a sound drubbing to the wicked, he would frequently be embarrassed in his choice, and would find, that the merits and demerits of most men and women scarcely amount to the value of either.

To suppose measures of approbation and blame, different from the human, confounds every thing. Whence do we learn, that there is such a thing as moral distinctions but from our own sentiments?

What man, who has not met with personal provocation (or what good natur'd man who has) could inflict on crimes, from the sense of blame alone, even the common, legal, frivolous punishments? And does any thing steel the breast of judges and juries against the sentiments of humanity but reflections on necessity and public interest?

By the Roman law, those who had been guilty of parricide and confessed their crime, were put into a sack, along with an ape, a dog, and a serpent; and thrown into the river: Death alone was the punishment of those, who denied their guilt, however fully proved. A criminal was tryed before Augustus, and condemned after full conviction: But the humane emperor, when he put the last interrogatory, gave it such a turn as to lead the wretch into a denial of his guilt. You surely, said the prince, did not kill your father. This lenity suits our natural ideas of RIGHT, even towards the greatest of all criminals, and even tho' it prevents so inconsiderable a sufferance. Nay, even the most bigotted priest would naturally, without reflection, approve of it; provided the crime was not heresy or infidelity. For as these crimes hurt himself in his temporal interests and advantages; perhaps he may not be altogether so indulgent to them.

The chief source of moral ideas is the reflection on the interests of human society. Ought these interests, so short, so frivolous, to be guarded by punishments, eternal and infinite? The damnation of one man is an infinitely greater evil in the universe, than the subversion of a thousand million of kingdoms.

Nature has rendered human infancy peculiarly frail and mortal; as it were on purpose to refute the notion of a probationary state. The half of mankind dye before they are rational creatures.

III. The physical arguments from the analogy of nature are strong for the mortality of the soul; and these are really the only philosophical arguments, which ought to be admitted with regard to this question, or indeed any question of fact.

Where any two objects are so closely connected, that all alterations, which we have ever seen in the one, are attended with proportionable alterations in the other; we ought to conclude, by all rules of analogy, that, when there are still greater alterations produced in the former, and it is totally dissolved, there follows a total dissolution of the latter.

Sleep, a very small effect on the body, is attended with a temporary extinction; at least, a great confusion in the soul.

The weakness of the body and that of the mind in infancy are exactly proportioned; their vigor in manhood; their sympathetic disorder in sickness; their common gradual decay in old age. The step farther seems unavoidable; their common dissolution in death.

The last symptoms, which the mind discovers, are disorder, weakness, insensibility, stupidity, the forerunners of its annihilation. The farther progress of the same causes, encreasing the same effects, totally extinguish it.

Judging by the usual analogy of nature, no form can continue, when transferred to a condition of life very different from the original one, in which it was placed. Trees perish in the water; fishes in the air; animals in the earth. Even so small a difference as that of climate is often fatal. What reason then to imagine, that an immense alteration, such as is made on the soul by the dissolution of its body and all its organs of thought and sensation, can be effected without the dissolution of the whole?

Every thing is in common between soul and body. The organs of the one are all of them the organs of the other. The existence therefore of the one must be dependent on that of the other.

The souls of animals are allowed to be mortal; and these bear so near a resemblance to the souls of men, that the analogy from one to the other forms a very strong argument. Their bodies are not more resembling; yet no one rejects the arguments drawn from comparative anatomy. The Metempsychosis is therefore the only system of this kind, that philosophy can so much as hearken to.

Nothing in this world is perpetual. Every being, however seemingly firm, is in continual flux and change: The world itself gives symptoms of frailty and dissolution: How contrary to analogy, therefore, to imagine, that one single form, seemingly the frailest of any, and from the slightest causes, subject, to the greatest disorders, is immortal and indissoluble? What a daring theory is that! How lightly, not to say, how rashly entertained!

How to dispose of the infinite number of posthumous existences ought also to embarrass the religious theory. Every planet, in every solar system, we are at liberty to imagine peopled with intelligent, mortal beings: At least, we can fix on no other supposition. For these, then, a new universe must, every generation, be created, beyond the bounds of the present universe; or one must have been created at first so prodigiously wide as to admit of this continual influx of beings. Ought such bold suppositions to be received by any philosophy; and that merely on pretence of a bare possibility?

When it is asked, whether Agamemnon, Thersites, Hannibal, Nero, and every stupid clown, that ever existed in Italy, Scythia, Bactria, or Guinea, are now alive; can any man think, that a scrutiny of nature will furnish arguments strong enough to answer so strange a question in the affirmative? The want of arguments, without revelation, sufficiently establishes the negative.

Quanto facilius, says Pliny, certiusque sibi quemque credere, ac specimen securitatis antigenitali sumere experimento. Our insensibility, before the composition of the body, seems to natural reason a proof of a like state after its dissolution.

Were our horror of annihilation an original passion, not the effect of our general love of happiness, it would rather prove the mortality of the soul. For as nature does nothing in vain, she would never give us a horror against an impossible event. She may give us a horror against an unavoidable event, provided our endeavours, as in the present case, may often remove it to some distance. Death is in the end unavoidable; yet the human species could not be preserved, had not nature inspired us with an aversion towards it.

All doctrines are to be suspected, which are favoured by our passions. And the hopes and fears which give rise to this doctrine, are very obvious.

It is an infinite advantage in every controversy, to defend the negative. If the question be out of the common experienced course of nature, this circumstance is almost, if not altogether, decisive. By what arguments or analogies can we prove any state of existence, which no one ever saw, and which no wise resembles any that ever was seen? Who will repose such trust in any pretended philosophy, as to admit upon its testimony the reality of so marvellous a scene? Some new species of logic is requisite for that purpose; and some new faculties of the mind, which may enable us to comprehend that logic.

Nothing could set in a fuller light the infinite obligations, which mankind have to divine revelation; since we find, that no other medium could ascertain this great and important truth..

APPENDIX C

C. OF SUICIDE

David Hume
Posthumous Publication

One considerable advantage, that arises from philosophy, consists in the sovereign antidote, which it affords to superstition and false religion. All other remedies against that pestilent distemper are vain, or, at least, uncertain. Plain good-sense, and the practice of the world, which alone serve most purposes of life, are here found ineffectual: History, as well as daily experience, affords instances of men, endowed with the strongest capacity for business and affairs, who have all their lives crouched under slavery to the grossest superstition. Even gaiety and sweetness of temper, which infuse a balm into every other wound, afford no remedy to so virulent a poison; as we may particularly observe of the fair sex, who, tho' commonly possessed of these rich presents of nature, feel many of their joys blasted by this importunate intruder. But when sound philosophy has once gained possession of the mind, superstition is effectually excluded; and one may safely affirm, that her triumph over this enemy is more compleat than over most of the vices and imperfections, incident to human nature. Love or anger, ambition or avarice, have their root in the temper and affections, which the soundest reason is scarce ever able fully to correct. But superstition, being founded on false opinion, must immediately vanish, when true philosophy has inspired juster sentiments of superior powers. The contest is here more equal between the distemper and the medicine: And nothing can hinder the latter from proving effectual, but its being false and sophisticated.

It will here be superfluous to magnify the merits of philosophy, by displaying the pernicious tendency of that vice, of which it cures the human mind. The superstitious man, says Tully, [Cicero, On Divination 2.72.] is miserable in every scene, in every incident of life. Even sleep itself, which banishes all other cares of unhappy mortals, affords to him matter of new terror; while he examines his dreams, and finds in those visions of the night, prognostications of future calamities. I may add, that, tho' death alone can put a full period to his misery, he dares not fly to this refuge, but still prolongs a miserable existence, from a vain fear, lest he offend his maker, by using the power, with which that beneficent being has endowed him. The presents of God and Nature are ravished from us by this cruel enemy; and notwithstanding that one step would remove us from the regions of pain and sorrow, her menaces still chain us down to a hated being, which she herself chiefly contributes to render miserable.

It is observed of such as have been reduced by the calamities of life to the necessity of employing this fatal remedy, that, if the unseasonable care of their friends deprive them of that species of death, which they proposed to themselves, they seldom venture upon any other, or can summon up so much resolution, a second time, as to execute their purpose. So great is our horror of death, that when it presents itself under any form, besides that to which a man has endeavoured to reconcile his imagination, it acquires new terrors, and overcomes his feeble courage. But when the menaces of superstition are joined to this natural timidity, no wonder it quite deprives men of all power over their lives; since even many pleasures and enjoyments, to which we are carried by a strong propensity, are torn from us by this inhuman tyrant. Let us here endeavour to restore men to their native liberty, by examining all the common arguments against Suicide, and shewing, that That action may be free from every imputation of guilt or blame; according to the sentiments of all the antient philosophers.

If Suicide be criminal, it must be a transgression of our duty, either to God, our neighbour, or ourselves.

To prove, that Suicide is no transgression of our duty to God, the following considerations may perhaps suffice. In order to govern the material world, the almighty creator has established general and immutable laws, by which all bodies, from the greatest planet to the smallest particle of matter, are maintained in their proper sphere and function. To govern the animal world, he has endowed all living creatures with bodily and mental powers; with senses, passions, appetites, memory, and judgment; by which they are impelled or regulated in that course of life, to which they are destined. These two distinct principles of the material and animal world continually encroach upon each other, and mutually retard or forward each other's operation. The powers of men and of all other animals are restrained and directed by the nature and qualities of the surrounding bodies; and the modifications and actions of these bodies are incessantly altered by the operation of all animals. Man is stopped by rivers in his passage over the surface of the earth; and rivers, when properly directed, lend their force to the motion of machines, which serve to the use of man. But tho' the provinces of the material and animal powers are not kept entirely separate, there result from thence no discord or disorder in the creation: On the contrary, from the mixture, union, and contrast of all the various powers of inanimate bodies and living creatures, arises that surprizing harmony and proportion, which affords the surest argument of supreme wisdom.

The providence of the deity appears not immediately in any operation, but governs every thing by those general and immutable laws, which have been established from the beginning of time. All events, in one sense, may be pronounced the action of the almighty: They all proceed from those powers, with which he has endowed his creatures. A house, which falls by its own weight, is not brought to ruin by his providence more than one destroyed by the hands of men; nor are the human faculties less his workmanship than the laws of motion and gravitation. When the passions play, when the judgment dictates, when the limbs obey; this is all the operation of God; and upon these animate principles, as well as upon the inanimate, has he established the government of the universe.

Every event is alike important in the eyes of that infinite being, who takes in, at one glance, the most distant regions of space and remotest periods of time. There is no one event, however important to us, which he has exempted from the general laws that govern the universe, or which he has peculiarly reserved for his own immediate action and operation. The revolutions of states and empires depend upon the smallest caprice or passion of single men; and the lives of men are shortened or extended by the smallest accident of air or diet, sunshine or tempest. Nature still continues her progress and operation; and if general laws be ever broke by particular volitions of the deity, 'tis after a manner which entirely escapes human observation. As on the one hand, the elements and other inanimate parts of the creation carry on their action without regard to the particular interest and situation of men; so men are entrusted to their own judgment and discretion in the various shocks of matter, and may employ every faculty, with which they are endowed, in order to provide for their ease, happiness, or preservation.

What is the meaning, then, of that principle, that a man, who, tired of life, and hunted by pain and misery, bravely overcomes all the natural terrors of death, and makes his escape from this cruel scene; that such a man, I say, has incurred the indignation of his creator, by encroaching on the office of divine providence, and disturbing the order of the universe? Shall we assert, that the Almighty has reserved to himself, in any peculiar manner, the disposal of the lives of men, and has not submitted that event, in common with others, to the general laws, by which the universe is governed? This is plainly false. The lives of men depend upon the same laws as the lives of all other animals; and these are subjected to the general laws of matter and motion. The fall of a tower or the infusion of a poison will destroy a man equally with the meanest creature: An inundation sweeps away every thing, without distinction, that comes within the reach of its fury. Since therefore the lives of men are for ever dependent on the general laws of matter and motion; is a man's disposing of his life criminal, because, in every case, it is criminal to encroach upon these laws, or disturb their operation? But this seems absurd. All animals are entrusted to their own prudence and skill for their conduct in the world, and have full authority, as far as their power extends, to alter all the operations of nature. Without the exercise of this authority, they could not subsist a moment. Every action, every motion of a man innovates in the order of some parts of matter, and diverts, from their ordinary course, the general laws of motion. Putting together, therefore, these conclusions, we find, that human life depends upon the general laws of matter and motion, and that 'tis no encroachment on the office of providence to disturb or alter these general laws. Has not every one, of consequence, the free disposal of his own life? And may he not lawfully employ that power with which nature has endowed him?

In order to destroy the evidence of this conclusion, we must shew a reason, why this particular case is excepted. Is it because human life is of so great importance, that it is a presumption for human prudence to dispose of it? But the life of man is of no greater importance to the universe than that of an oyster. And were it of ever so great importance, the order of nature has actually submitted it to human prudence, and reduced us to a necessity, in every incident, of determining concerning it.

Were the disposal of human life so much reserved as the peculiar province of the almighty that it were an encroachment on his right for men to dispose of their own lives; it would be equally criminal to act for the preservation of life as for its destruction. If I turn aside a stone, which is falling upon my head, I disturb the course of nature, and I invade the peculiar province of the almighty, by lengthening out my life, beyond the period, which, by the general laws of matter and motion, he had assigned to it.

A hair, a fly, an insect is able to destroy this mighty being, whose life is of such importance. Is it an absurdity to suppose, that human prudence may lawfully dispose of what depends on such insignificant causes?

It would be no crime in me to divert the Nile or Danube from its course, were I able to effect such purposes. Where then is the crime of turning a few ounces of blood from their natural chanels!

Do you imagine that I repine at providence or curse my creation, because I go out of life, and put a period to a being, which, were it to continue, would render me miserable? Far be such sentiments from me. I am only convinced of a matter of fact, which you yourself acknowledge possible, that human life may be unhappy, and that my existence, if farther prolonged, would become uneligible. But I thank providence, both for the good, which I have already enjoyed, and for the power, with which I am endowed, of escaping the ill that threatens me.[Agamus Deo gratias, quod nemo in vita teneri potest. Seneca, Epist. xii.] To you it belongs to repine at providence, who foolishly imagine that you have no such power, and who must still prolong a hated being, tho' loaded with pain and sickness, with shame and poverty.

Do you not teach, that when any ill befalls me, tho' by the malice of my enemies, I ought to be resigned to providence; and that the actions of men are the operations of the almighty as much as the actions of inanimate beings? When I fall upon my own sword, therefore, I receive my death equally from the hands of the deity, as if it had proceeded from a lion, a precipice, or a fever.

The submission, which you require to providence, in every calamity, that befalls me, excludes not human skill and industry; if possibly, by their means, I can avoid or escape the calamity. And why may I not employ one remedy as well as another?

If my life be not my own, it were criminal for me to put it in danger, as well as to dispose of it: Nor could one man deserve the appellation of Hero, whom glory or friendship transports into the greatest dangers, and another merit the reproach of Wretch or Miscreant, who puts a period to his life, from the same or like motives.

There is no being, which possesses any power or faculty, that it receives not from its creator; nor is there any one, which, by ever so irregular an action, can encroach upon the plan of his providence, or disorder the universe. Its operations are his work equally with that chain of events, which it invades; and which ever principle prevails, we may, for that very reason, conclude it to be most favoured by him. Be it animate or inanimate, rational or irrational, 'tis all a case: It's power is still derived from the supreme creator, and is alike comprehended in the order of his providence. When the horror of pain prevails over the love of life: When a voluntary action anticipates the effect of blind causes; it is only in consequence of those powers and principles, which he has implanted in his creatures. Divine providence is still inviolate, and placed far beyond the reach of human injuries.

It is impious, says the old Roman superstition, [Tacit. Ann. lib. i.] to divert rivers from their course, or invade the prerogatives of nature. 'Tis impious, says the French superstition, to inoculate for the small-pox, or usurp the business of providence, by voluntarily producing distempers and maladies. 'Tis impious, says the modern European superstition, to put a period to our own life, and thereby rebel against our creator. And why not impious, say I, to build houses, cultivate the ground, and sail upon the ocean? In all these actions, we employ our powers of mind and body to produce some innovation in the course of nature; and in none of them do we any more. They are all of them, therefore, equally innocent or equally criminal.

But you are placed by providence, like a sentinel, in a particular station; and when you desert it, without being recalled, you are guilty of rebellion against your almighty sovereign, and have incurred his displeasure. I ask, why do you conclude, that Providence has placed me in this station? For my part, I find, that I owe my birth to a long chain of causes, of which many and even the principal, depended upon voluntary actions of men. But Providence guided all these causes, and nothing happens in the universe without its consent and co-operation. If so, then neither does my death, however voluntary, happen without it's consent; and whenever pain and sorrow so far overcome my patience as to make me tired of life, I may conclude, that I am recalled from my station, in the clearest and most express terms.

It is providence, surely, that has placed me at present in this chamber: But may I not leave it, when I think proper, without being liable to the imputation of having deserted my post or station? When I shall be dead, the principles, of which I am composed, will still perform their part in the universe, and will be equally useful in the grand fabric, as when they composed this individual creature. The difference to the whole will be no greater than between my being in a chamber and in the open air. The one change is of more importance to me than the other; but not more so to the universe.

It is a kind of blasphemy to imagine, that any created being can disturb the order of the world, or invade the business of providence. It supposes, that that being possesses powers and faculties, which it received not from its creator, and which are not subordinate to his government and authority. A man may disturb society, no doubt; and thereby incur the displeasure of the almighty: But the government of the world is placed far beyond his reach and violence. And how does it appear, that the almighty is displeased with those actions, that disturb society? By the principles which he has implanted in human nature, and which inspire us with a sentiment of remorse, if we ourselves have been guilty of such actions, and with that of blame and disapprobation, if we ever observe them in others. Let us now examine, according to the method proposed, whether Suicide be of this kind of actions, and be a breach of our duty to our neighbour and to society.

A man, who retires from life, does no harm to society. He only ceases to do good; which, if it be an injury, is of the lowest kind.

All our obligations to do good to society seem to imply something reciprocal. I receive the benefits of society, and therefore ought to promote it's interest. But when I withdraw myself altogether from society, can I be bound any longer?

But allowing, that our obligations to do good were perpetual, they have certainly some bounds. I am not obliged to do a small good to society, at the expence of a great harm to myself. Why then should I prolong a miserable existence, because of some frivolous advantage, which the public may, perhaps, receive from me? If upon account of age and infirmities, I may lawfully resign any office, and employ my time altogether in fencing against these calamities, and alleviating, as much as possible, the miseries of my future life: Why may I not cut short these miseries at once by an action, which is no more prejudicial to society?

But suppose, that it is no longer in my power to promote the interest of the public: Suppose, that I am a burthen to it: Suppose, that my life hinders some person from being much more useful to the public. In such cases my resignation of life must not only be innocent but laudable. And most people, who lie under any temptation to abandon existence, are in some such situation. Those, who have health, or power, or authority, have commonly better reason to be in humour with the world.

A man is engaged in a conspiracy for the public interest; is seized upon suspicion; is threatened with the rack; and knows, from his own weakness, that the secret will be extorted from him: Could such a one consult the public interest better than by putting a quick period to a miserable life? This was the case of the famous and brave Strozzi of Florence.

Again, suppose a malefactor justly condemned to a shameful death; can any reason be imagined, why he may not anticipate his punishment, and save himself all the anguish of thinking on its dreadful approaches? He invades the business of providence no more than the magistrate did, who ordered his execution; and his voluntary death is equally advantageous to society, by ridding it of a pernicious member.

That Suicide may often be consistent with interest and with our duty to ourselves, no one can question, who allows, that age, sickness, or misfortune may render life a burthen, and make it worse even than annihilation. I believe that no man ever threw away life, while it was worth keeping. For such is our natural horror of death, that small motives will never be able to reconcile us to it. And tho' perhaps the situation of a man's health or fortune did not seem to require this remedy, we may at least be assured, that any one, who, without apparent reason, has had recourse to it, was curst with such an incurable depravity or gloominess of temper, as must poison all enjoyment, and render him equally miserable as if he had been loaded with the most grievous misfortunes.

If Suicide be supposed a crime, 'tis only cowardice can impel us to it. If it be no crime, both prudence and courage should engage us to rid ourselves at once of existence, when it becomes a burthen. 'Tis the only way, that we can then be useful to society, by setting an example, which, if imitated, would preserve to every one his chance for happiness in life, and would effectually free him from all danger of misery.

It would be easy to prove, that Suicide is as lawful under the christian dispensation as it was to the heathens. There is not a single text of scripture, which prohibits it. That great and infallible rule of faith and practice, which must controul all philosophy and human reasoning, has left us, in this particular, to our natural liberty. Resignation to providence is, indeed, recommended in scripture; but that implies only submission to ills, which are unavoidable, not to such as may be remedied by prudence or courage. Thou shalt not kill is evidently meant to exclude only the killing of others, over whose life we have no authority. That this precept like most of the scripture precepts, must be modified by reason and common sense, is plain from the practice of magistrates, who punish criminals capitally, notwithstanding the letter of this law. But were this commandment ever so express against Suicide, it could now have no authority. For all the law of Moses is abolished, except so far as it is established by the law of nature; and we have already endeavoured to prove, that Suicide is not prohibited by that law. In all cases, Christians and Heathens are precisely upon the same footing; and if Cato and Brutus, Arria and Portia acted heroically, those who now imitate their example ought to receive the same praises from posterity. The power of committing Suicide is regarded by Pliny as an advantage which men possess even above the deity himself. Deus non sibi potest mortem consciscere, si velit, quod homini dedit optimum in tantis vitæ pœnis. Lib. ii. Cap. 7..

VIII GLOSSARY AND BIBLIOGRAPHY

GLOSSARY

Abstract reasoning A priori or deductive reasoning.

Analogical argument A species of a posteriori argument in which an analogy is drawn between the observed attributes of two things or events in order to prove the probability that some further similarity exists.

A posteriori argument An argument that is intended to give a degree of probability to the conclusion. Also known as an inductive argument. The term a posteriori is also used to refer to knowledge based on or derived from experience and observation.

A priori argument An argument that is intended to give certainty to the conclusion. A synonym is deductive. The term a priori is also used to refer to knowledge that is not based on or derived from experience.

Argumentum ad absurdum Also known as reduction to absurdity." A form of argument that attempts either to disprove a statement by showing it inevitably leads to a ridiculous, absurd, or impractical conclusion, or to prove one by showing that if it were not true, the result would be absurd or impossible. See Wikipedia for examples https://en.wikipedia.org/wiki/Reductio_ad_absurdum .

Begging the question A fallacy in which the author of an argument wrongly assumes that a relevant question has received an affirmative answer.

Cosmological argument An argument for the existence of God derived from the factual claim that every event has a cause.

Counter example In logic, a counter example to an argument is a substitution instance of its form where the premises are all true and the conclusion is false.

Deductive argument See a priori.

Demonstrable A proposition is demonstrable if it can be proven to be true with certainty

Design Argument An inductive argument for the existence and nature of God that uses the similarity of natural objects to machines as the basis for concluding that both have their origin in the work of an intelligent designer.

Experimental principle In Hume's writings, the experimental principle is "Like effects prove like causes."

Finite deity A deity that whose attributes are limited, e.g. having intelligence that may be superior to the intelligence of any human being, but whose intelligence is not infinitely superior.

Immortality of the soul The belief that the human soul exists prior to the birth of the human body and will to continue to exist after the death of the human body.

Inductive argument See a posteriori.

Infinite deity A deity/god whose perfection is without limits, e.g. all-good, omnipotent and omniscient.

Law of nature Hume also uses the phrase "general laws of matter and motion." These are descriptive, not prescriptive laws. They describe regularities that are observable in natural occurrences, e.g. the motion of the planets, the temperature at which water freezes.

Metaphysical topics Arguments used to prove the immortality of the soul, and founded on "the supposition that the soul is immaterial, and that it is impossible for thought to belong to a material substance."

Miracle Hume's definition: "A transgression of a law of nature by a particular volition of the deity, or by the interposition of some invisible agent."

Monotheism Belief in one god.

Moral evil Man-made evil, for example, the Holocaust.

Moral topics Arguments used to prove the immortality of the soul by derivation from "the justice of God."

Natural evil Harm caused by natural events, for example, deaths and injuries due to hurricanes, floods, and wildfires.

Natural religion Religious beliefs supported by scientific evidence and reasoning (compare "revealed religion").

Necessary existence A being is necessarily existent when existence is part of the concept or definition of that being.

Ontological argument An a priori argument for the existence of God derived from the definition or concept of God.

Physical topics Arguments used by Hume to prove the mortality of the soul; these arguments are founded on the analogy of nature (see analogical argument).

Polytheism Belief in many gods.

Probability Probability refers to evidence founded on past experience in which the conjunction between two objects or events has been found to be variable. Compare "proof."

Problem of evil How can the existence of God (defined as a being who is all-perfect) be made consistent with the existence of evil?

Proof A proof is evidence founded on past experience in which the conjunction between two objects or events has been found to be "constant". Compare "probability."

Revealed religion Religious beliefs derived from the revelations of a deity. (Compare "natural religion")

Theism Belief in one god who is the creator of the universe and who has every perfection (all-good, all-wise, all-powerful, eternal, and self-existent)

Theogony The genealogy of a group or system of gods.

Thought experiment An experiment of the mind or imagination, usually employed in philosophy to disprove a theory or principle by showing that it leads to an unacceptable or contradictory conclusion. (Compare argumentum ad absurdum arguments). See examples at https://www.toptenz.net/top-10-most-famous-thought-experiments.php

BIBLIOGRAPHY

A complete bibliography of 668 articles and books on Hume's philosophy of religion can be found at PhilPapers:
https://philpapers.org/browse/hume-philosophy-of-religion

The bibliography is divided into several useful subcategories:

Hume: The Argument from Evil (13)

Hume: Atheism (27)

Hume: Design Arguments for Theism (45)

Hume: Cosmological Arguments for Theism (13)

Hume: Philosophy of Religion, Misc (164)

Hume's Argument against Miracles (195)

ABOUT LAURENCE HOULGATE

Laurence Houlgate is Emeritus Professor of Philosophy at California Polytechnic State University in San Luis Obispo, California. He received M.A. and Ph.D. degrees in philosophy at the University of California, Los Angeles. He has previously held professorships at the University of California, Santa Barbara, and George Mason University. In addition to books in the *Smart Student's Guide* series, he has published articles on moral and legal responsibility in philosophical and law journals and is the author of four books on topics in the philosophy of family law: *The Child and the State*; *Philosophy, Law and the Family*; and *Morals, Marriage and Parenthood*.

Made in the USA
Coppell, TX
20 April 2023